Job Search = Love Search
10 Savvy Career Strategies That
Help You Find Love Too

E. Elizabeth Carter

&

Ronnie Ann Ryan

Published by The Charmed Press, LLC
All orders and inquiries for *Job Search = Love Search*
should be addressed to:
Ronnie Ann Ryan
P. O. Box 417
Milford, CT 06460

ISBN: 0-9767991-3-8

First edition.

Printed in the United States of America.

Cover designed by Stacey Slimak Shea.

Disclaimer

This book is intended for informational and educational
purposes only. It is not meant to provide counseling or
medical advice.

Contents

Introduction

A few summers ago, I was sitting on the couch in Beth's office talking as usual about dating and coaching. Dating coaching is what I do - helping women over 40 find love. I met Beth when I spoke to a singles group she ran and we hit it off. Beth and I stayed in touch, having lunch every now and then for fun.

With trays of take-out sushi sitting on the table before us, we caught up on life and summer plans. But this one particular afternoon, we stumbled on an idea - something we could work on together which got us incredibly excited.

We started discussing my theory on how looking for love is so similar to looking for a job. Beth, an executive recruiter and certified career coach, jumped on this immediately and the idea for this book was born. Birthed from salmon avocado rolls and tuna with spicy sauce, smothered with wasabi, soy sauce, and ginger.

Beth got a couple of pads of paper and pens (we are traditionalists) and the ideas emerged at a frenetic pace amidst peals of laughter. We were having so much fun coming up with all the parallels and how many career strategies could really work to attract a romantic partner as well.

More than three years later, we have finally finished our labor of love (and career). The end product is a savvy guide packed with 10 smart career strategies that can also be used to help you find love.

As a dating coach, I see opportunities to apply dating strategies all the time in my own life, even though I've been married since May 2000. Somehow, my work still mimics what I went through on my dating journey to find my adorable husband.

Whatever I'm going through, looking for new clients, seeking business partners, I still get excited and hopeful, and then rejected and shut down. The perils of dating are all still there for me, just in a different format. As a result, I continue to refer to my own dating strategies and theories since they work for me now in other areas of life.

The same thing goes for executive recruiting and career coaching. Beth has seen it all. She shares stories that are funny and sometimes painful recruiting assignments she has completed. In many instances, she also turns to her own career and coaching advice to navigate a variety of non-career situations she comes up against.

That's the long way of saying our combined suggestions can help with a multitude of circumstances in your life beyond career and dating, so you'll get plenty of value from the content we put forth.

We hope you take advantage of our combined wisdom and knowledge for either goal or maybe both! Regardless of which path you pursue, we hope this book helps with your journey to handle the twists and turns that happen along the way. Embrace it all and go for what you want most.

JOB SEARCH = LOVE SEARCH

1

Career & Dating Strategy

▪ Beth - Executive Recruiter & Career Coach

Are you a planner? Do you look into your options and think about what you want?

How many times have you planned a vacation? Not only do you have to figure out where you are going but you have to consider logistics. You might plan what you are going to do for entertainment as well as food and lodging. Cost is another consideration. Some people plan their vacations to the minute while others just pick a place and wing it.

Do you have a financial plan that may include saving for retirement, children's college funds, and/or other estate issues? Maybe you work with a financial advisor that guides you on the various instruments you can use to invest your money, the amount of risk you are willing to take, and what time frames will work best for you.

What about a life plan? Have you ever spent the time to plan out what you want in life? Most people answer "No" to this when I ask during my presentations. Without a life plan, it is difficult to create an effective career strategy.

By analyzing the different facets of your life, you can start to develop a vision for what you want in the future. You may want to consider creating a vision board or a scrapbook that includes photos or pictures of things you want out of life including the house you want to own, a specific car you want to buy, or a place you want to visit.

The different parts of the life plan should include the following sections: body, personal growth, physical surroundings, family and friends, significant other, career, and money. I used to have "fun" as a separate category, but someone pointed out that there should be some element of fun in everything we do or we will not be motivated to continue. I agree and try to encourage my clients to realize that fun is necessary even with their job. Fun can help foster creative ideas and a much more enjoyable work environment.

Your health is very important and that fact is certainly well documented. When looking for a new position, it really helps to maintain a healthy diet and get proper exercise. The job search can be a very stressful time so use your downtime to take a walk, relax, or do one of your favorite hobbies. Make sure you get enough sleep too. You need every advantage to be at the top of your game.

Once you land a job, you can't stop taking time for yourself then either. The easiest way to continue your self-care is to carve time out early in the morning or after work. Or you may prefer actually "scheduling" it during the day just like you would do with any other appointment. If you analyze your week and determine when you are full of energy and when you are not, you can probably come up with at least one or more times that you can take a solid break to go to the gym or just take a walk outside of the office. These breaks are not only good for the body but also the mind. Keeping yourself refreshed allows you to tackle your duties much more effectively.

When I interview candidates, I ask what they are doing for professional development. Most say they don't have the time to take a class. There are often other options such as participating in a teleclass or webinar, reading a "how to" book, or registering for a live seminar. Even attending a networking event can be fruitful because you can learn from other people – their mannerisms, how they engage others, and how they market their products, services, and even themselves! To really grow as a person, continuous learning is the key to success. As my grandmother who lived to 103 said, "When you stop learning, you stop living."

Physical surroundings need to be addressed because not only does it reflect who you are but it also can make for a productive work environment or a calming home.

As an example, a friend of mine convinced me to paint my living room and dining room walls a sunny yellow. Once the paint had dried, I really questioned this because the rooms were so bright you felt like you needed to wear sunglasses. Once we put pictures and curtains up and added the furniture and rugs, the rooms became very welcoming and cozy.

Ironically, the paint was called Pure Joy and I felt that way every time I walked into those rooms or entertained my friends and family. Many people work in cubicles but that does not mean they have to be sterile looking and not portray the person who works there for many hours every week. It still is necessary to make the space productive, but adding calming or cheerful pictures, family photos or other mementos that make you feel good will be beneficial.

How does this fit into a job search strategy? If you are the type of person that needs to work in a very quiet space and the position you are looking at requires you to be in a loud workplace or share an office or cubicle, it may not be the right place for you to work. Many people would try to make it work but noise and chatty co-workers can be very disruptive, causing you a lot of stress. Definitely spend the time looking at the space you would be working in before you accept the offer.

Family and friends are a huge factor in your job search strategy. Putting aside positions that would require relocation and totally change the family lifestyle, other important factors need to be considered when seeking a new position. If you have children, their different stages of development affect your stage in your career. Although little ones need more supervision, they also tend to have less problems. As one person recently said, "Little kids, little problems, big kids, bigger problems."

As children age, you may have more free time in terms of hours, but you also have to deal with issues like peer pressure, lots of homework, college applications, and just the trials and tribulations of being a teenager. If you need to travel a lot for your position or spend many hours in the office, you have to either devise creative ways to be there for your children or realize that in this stage of your life, this is not the right role for you. During negotiations, you can ask for work at home arrangements or blackout periods when you will not travel. Be cautious because many employers are not that flexible.

Spouses need to be consulted because the family dynamics may be affected. Your partner needs to agree to the new changes. Think about all logistics. Will you need a ride to the train station, have to shift your normal dinner time, or need your home to be quiet for those days you work at home? You'd need to think about pets, landscapers, and other noises and distractions and keep them to a minimum for those days, to maintain a professional environment, especially during conference calls. Many frustrations I deal with as a career coach come from not having a frank conversation about the expectations for a new position and how it will affect things outside of the office.

The spouse also has to have a clear understanding of the search process and most importantly BE PATIENT! I had one client who was sitting in my office telling me how his search was going. Occasionally he looked up as he spoke and after the third time I stopped him and asked him why he was doing this. He said rather sadly that his wife is a realtor so relied on him for health benefits. She had her office in the house that was upstairs from where my client was conducting his job search. She was very scared that he would not find a job soon so they would need to find reasonably priced health insurance. She was relentless in asking each day how things were going which did not help his stress level. For a man over six feet tall, you could tell he was scared of his wife.

Friends can also be a factor when looking for a job. Some can be very helpful and serve as advocates to connect with you potential employers. Others can actually sabotage your search efforts. The key factor is communication. You need to explain fully what you are looking for in a new role and what the deal breakers are.

This can be challenging because your friends, like your family, have their own thoughts on "what is best for you." You'll need to take time to describe your ideal role, the types of people you work best with, the best work environment for you, and if you are open to relocation among other details. In addition, give examples of things that have not worked well for you in the past that could include projects for which you did not have the right skills or resources or a boss that was condescending and unsupportive.

We work to earn a living. That's why money needs to be explored in terms of what your minimum compensation can be and what other perks you may receive in lieu of base and bonus. Other things to consider include the commute, clothing, phone and travel expenses, and computer equipment. Your last job may have required an hour-long commute each way and you needed to dress in business attire every day. Besides gas and maintenance on your car, you may also have had big dry cleaning costs.

Now picture your next position as one that is five minutes from your home with casual attire. Think how much money you would save. That can really add up! In addition, determine what your per hour cost is and how much more free time you will have which could be used to clean your home, mow your lawn, and spend more time with your children versus day care. Plus, how much money will you save if you do these things yourself?

Once you determine your new budget, you can negotiate more effectively. You earn a bit less money but also work less hours and have more free time. Other perks could be a health club membership and other health-related expenses, extra vacation time, trip rewards, concierge service, take home meals, on-site daycare, and bring your pet to work.

Although there are many considerations that need to be explored, planning your career strategy can be a great time for self-reflection and visualizing what your future will be. Needless to say, these areas will change over time as children age, your needs change, new challenges are sought after, new skills are learned, and the workplace evolves. By periodically re-evaluating where you are today and where you want to be in later years, you can devise and revise your career strategy more effectively.

♥ Ronnie - Dating Coach

Dating Strategy

Just like with a life plan, it helps to have a dating plan and that starts with being honest with yourself about your love life agenda. Do you want to marry? Do you want to start a family? Do you want to live together or prefer a committed relationship living separately? Or are you simply looking for casual companionship and nothing serious?

This may seem silly or over the top to you, but knowing what you want and having a plan is essential to finding the right type of partner. Here's why. Let's say you just want to be casual and aren't ready for something serious. So you start dating single people who also aren't looking for anything serious. Over time, you somehow find yourself having fallen in love. Now you feel more serious. Trouble is, you met your partner under the guise of being casual. So, even though your own intentions have changed, the other person probably is happy to keep things as they are. Now you have a big problem.

I have found many of my dating coaching clients are not honest with themselves. They don't believe they can find true love, so they convince themselves they don't really want that or need it. Yet, once you spend enough time with a guy and enjoy his company, feelings grow.

Too bad that change in your love agenda doesn't usually go over well with Mr. Casual. He wants nothing to do with that and hasn't changed his desire for anything more serious. The reasons for this are endless, such as having a difficult divorce, being cheated on, or just enjoying his freedom. Yet, the reasons why do not matter. What matters is his agenda is not the same as yours and you will not get him to change that.

To avoid this situation, spend quiet time really thinking about what you want. Be honest with yourself. If you want love, admit it. You should go for what is your heart's desire. Whatever you decide, know that switching gears and going from casual to serious often doesn't happen naturally as you get older. Maybe it did when you were 22, but it's not so likely when you are 40 and over.

It also pays to envision the type of lifestyle you want. If you want to travel, don't fall for a homebody. If you want to dine out and enjoy gourmet food, don't expect a man who likes burgers to be the right match. I have seen this time and time again where women try to mold a man to meet their needs. It usually has a disastrous ending ranging from breaking up and heartache to finding yourself in divorce court. You cannot change a man - he is who he is right now.

When you know what you want, then seek a man who fits with your vision and lifestyle. You will get along better and enjoy each other more. Or, decide what is vital to you and be clear about your deal breakers. For example, you may not want a man who smokes, is not yet divorced, doesn't share the same religious, or political views or drinks more than you do.

On the other hand, consider those things you are willing to bend on and compromise. This helps make room for a man who doesn't meet every little need, but matches the big picture. The more leeway you are open to, the better your chances of finding a good partner. Whatever you decide, don't kid yourself and then end up heartbroken.

Lastly, know that there are many ways to handle the money in a relationship. Sometimes you split things evenly. Others divide the expenses with one person paying the mortgage and the other covering the food, electricity and other household expenses. A third option is to pay proportionally based on your comparative wages.

What you are willing to do to pay for expenses of the life you want? Think this through now, before you are in a relationship and that will help things go so much smoother later. The more flexible you are, the more easily you can blend two households. Knowing what you might be willing to do with the right man can help pave the way later. It's all part of the planning process.

Dating Lesson

According to Dictionary.com, one definition for the word strategy is, "a plan, method, or series of maneuvers...for obtaining a specific goal or result." Given that, ask yourself, what do you want to achieve by dating and more importantly, how do you plan to get there?

The issue with most goal setting and strategy development, particularly when it comes to dating, is that people tend to be vague. The goal might be, "I want to meet the right man." That is all well and good, but the likelihood of you succeeding is slim without more details and a strong plan.

Instead, invest time getting clear on what you want and visualize that. Create a vision board, make a scrapbook, or write down the specifics in a journal to help you define the things you really want.

Regarding dating, a strategy goes far beyond a man's physical appeal (although you may have preferences for height, build, and hair or lack of it). More importantly, this is an opportunity to figure out what kind of person you want to spend your life with which is about a man's character. Also, consider what your romantic partner means to you, how you will get along, and how you will spend time together. Your vision board may include two people walking hand-in-hand through a park, traveling to exotic places, or cooking a meal together.

To me, the best television commercial that exemplifies this is an old one. Do you remember the ad for diamonds that stated, "A Diamond is Forever"? In the commercial, an older couple walks through a park holding hands. They are not talking, but you can see they love each other completely. A younger couple comes up behind them and the younger woman looks back at the older couple and smiles. This scenario brings to mind that you can be so in love with a person you don't need to be talking. You can simply be elated to be close and in each other's company.

When you put together your plan to find love, be as exact as you can. Spell out the number of days per month you'll do something to meet men and how many guys you'll email online per week to fill out your dating action plan.

Next, think about what the relationship involves. If you prefer a casual relationship, you may only want to go on a date every couple of weeks. For a committed relationship, figure out how many times a week you want to see the guy, how much talking and texting is desired and if you want daily contact.

What does your ideal relationship look like? Think ahead to see if that is realistic. It's good to know what you want and go for it. Yet, it's also important to be realistic or you could keep yourself single with no man being capable of jumping the bar you set.

Or the stumbling block could be something simple that isn't based in reality. You may want to see the person every day, but that won't be possible with your work schedule. The more details you define upfront, the easier it is to know if you've found "the one."

Of course, the best-laid plans do not always come to be. That's OK. Getting clear on what you want will help you get close and most people who go through this planning process find they end up with many of the items they specified.

I had one client, Kathryn, who did all sorts of things to bring love into her life. She was into spirituality, so she lit candles, said prayers, and made a vision map collage among other activities. Kathryn sat with me and cried about everything she had done to attract love into her life.

I was a bit puzzled since in my mind as a dating coach, she left something rather important out of her plan. I asked her what she actually did to meet men face-to-face. Surprisingly, she hadn't done anything. She was so busy attracting love by spiritual means into her life that she never actually went out to meet guys.

Men won't magically appear. You have to get out and cross paths with men to meet them and find a good match. Kathryn shifted her plan to include singles dances and online dating which as you can imagine, helped a lot to find the love she dreamed of.

2

Personal Branding—Know You're a Great Catch

Beth - Executive Recruiter & Career Coach

Before you start your job search, it is important to think about how you want to portray yourself to others. There have been many articles written about personal branding tailored to various groups including the job seeker, the celebrity, and even those in corporate environments. Unfortunately, most people read these articles and try to create their so-called image but fail - the result often does not truly reflect who they are. Instead, they end up sending a mixed message to others, actually muddying the waters about who they are and what they stand for. Needless to say, this can affect being chosen for a new job, a promotion, or even a business relationship.

How then do you create an accurate picture of yourself? I advise my clients to spend some time identifying their core values which create the foundation of their career and life. To clarify what is really important to you today and how you want your life to look in the future, you need to choose 5-7 core values that you will never compromise. If something happens that goes against your core values, this becomes a deal breaker.

After you establish your seven core values, rank them and choose the top four to work with. Write them down and think about how they interact. Some of my clients have even drawn circles with each value to discover where they overlap. Writing them down versus typing them on a computer is important because it has been proven that pencil/pen to paper has a greater impact on your psyche for achieving your goals.

The next step is to discuss with friends, family, coworkers, and possibly your boss if these core values are evident to others. Objective feedback is crucial to see if you are on target about your choices, but you'll need to be open to hearing what people have to say so that you don't become defensive when something disturbing or surprising comes up. This is a stage requiring serious reflection, so take as much time as needed. Ask open-ended questions and try to get the people you ask to cite specific examples of how they feel this value does or does not fit you. If it does not match, ask what other values they feel better suit you and why.

Compile these conversations and look for common themes or phrases. From this investigation, you can develop a personal mission statement that explains who you are. This is the foundation of your personal branding. The statement is usually in one or possibly two sentences and uses action words. Some questions to ponder while you are devising your personal mission statement are:

- Remember a time when something dramatically changed your life. What were the positive outcomes?

- If I had another chance I would…

- I wish I had the courage to…

- My legacy is/I want to be remembered for…

- What superhero/animal/fruit/insect would you be and why?

I am joking about the last question but it drives home the point that you need to think very broad.

Here's an example of a personal mission statement:

"To collaborate, motivate, empower, and challenge my coaching clients which will assist them in reaching their goals resulting in a positive impact on their organizations."

The next step is to craft a simple way to communicate your mission statement and convey who you are. This is called a "60 second commercial" which quickly sums up your branding in a memorable way. Chapter IV delves deeper into creating one. You will use this commercial during a career transition meeting, an interview, or even a voice mail you are leaving to a prospective employer.

I recommend that you test it out in front of the mirror, speaking the words out loud. Look at your facial expressions to notice how you come across. You want to reflect positive emotions such as feeling happy and confident versus sad or confused. Do not sound like a robot or a timid mouse. If your message does not flow easily, ask for help from some of the people you contacted before. The objective is not to make this "perfect" but for you to get your message across effectively and for you to be comfortable and at ease saying it. In addition, it is imperative for your advocates to be able to relay this message when speaking on your behalf.

Something that can really help you craft a strong personal pitch is to watch videos of prominent people in society – celebrities, athletes, and high profiled CEOs. Listen to the words they use and also watch their body language. Confident people who feel good about what they are saying, portray a self-assured persona. When they speak, others most likely listen intently and believe what is being said. On the other hand, insecure people tend to fidget and not maintain good eye contact which can lead others to think they lack confidence or worse, are hiding something. This is a classic interpretation of this type of body language.

If you make a life change, it will be necessary to revisit your personal brand to "tweak" it, ensuring the message continues to be an accurate reflection of who you are. Thinking back to past accomplishments and memorable "Aha! Moments" can also help you when revising your message. The recipe for success is to keep your branding and message simple and straightforward.

♥ Ronnie - Dating Coach

How You Present Yourself as a Date or Mate

You might not think you have to go to this extent to get a date for Saturday night. But the single woman who invests time learning about herself gets clear on what she has to offer and how to communicate that to men she meets.

With dating, branding and personal presentation have a similar intention as job hunting. First, understand that a man chooses a woman because she makes him feel good about himself. That's why it's to your advantage to be warm, friendly, easy to be with, confident, fun, and delightful. Sounds like the topics taught in finishing school, right? Turns out those social instructions are not just "fluff," but valuable knowledge and a skill set that can help you get ahead in dating, job hunting, and life.

With that in mind, during a first phone call, and then the first date, you want to be your very best self. Everything needs to consistently reflect who you are as a fabulous romantic partner.

Don't worry – you don't need to be thinking of each little detail every minute you are with a new guy. The point is to get the details down, so it becomes a natural part of who you are. When you know your personal brand, you actually make it easier to present yourself and eliminate the guesswork that pops up when you haven't done this essential self-reflection before dating.

Image

Let's start with your image which includes hair, makeup, nails and grooming, clothing styles, colors, and accessories.

Pampering – Most men like a woman who takes care of herself. I'm not talking about high maintenance – but a level of self-care that shows you value yourself. That says a lot about who you are. According to Mama Gena [Regina Thomashauser), a pampered woman is a happy woman. When you honor yourself by taking care of yourself, others will honor you too.

Even though you have a busy life with a career, children, elderly parents etc., you will have more to give when you take care of yourself first. This is a basic rule of thumb for any caregiver. It's like the instructions given on a plane about oxygen – moms are told to put their own oxygen masks on first and then help their children. If you just give and give without giving to yourself, you drain your energy and ability to help others.

The point is, make time to take care of yourself. This is about how you value yourself.

Hair – When was the last time you updated your hairstyle? To look youthful and current, ask your hairdresser for a new cut that suits your face and is easy to maintain. Color can also make a big difference. Covering the gray is important, but if you have dark hair, consider highlights or a lighter shade. As women age, dark hair can actually make you look older, whereas a lighter color adds vitality to your look. In addition, make sure you get your hair done on a regular basis so you always look good with no telltale grays frosting your part.

Makeup – Not all women wear makeup. But as you hit 40, a little color can bring back your youthful glow. It's OK to go basic. You can still achieve the natural look if you wear only mascara, blush and lipstick. The "basic three" as I call it will perk up your skin tone and highlight your features. Application takes less than five minutes, but takes years off your appearance.

Nails – If you don't like to fuss, you don't need long nails or colorful polish. As long as they are neat, well-shaped, and clean you are all set. On the other hand, manicured nails do send a message of a well-cared for woman, but it's not a must.

Clothing – So many of my dating coaching clients have two wardrobes – work clothing and casual clothes.

But, if you are a single woman looking for love, you also need a dating wardrobe! This includes outfits that make you feel attractive, alluring, and sexy. You don't need to wear plunging necklines and spandex to get attention. Instead, wear clothes that show off your assets because men are visual.

Every woman has her own style and I'm not taking away from that. But work clothes are often purposely not sexy and casual clothes are often not very flattering.

Savvy Clothing Tips for an Appealing Personal Presentation

1. Research shows men like red, pink, and coral. If you want to wear black, use these colors as accents. Choose colors that are flattering to your hair and skin tone.

2. Do you have great legs? Show them off in a skirt! You don't need to wear a short skirt but letting men see your legs when most women tend to wear pants is a savvy plan.

3. Small waistline? Wear belts to accentuate your curves.

4. Open necklines including scoop and "v" necks communicate non-verbally that you are open, as opposed to turtlenecks that cover your throat and collar bones. Your neck is the area for communication and

also an erogenous zone, which is why covering it up shortchanges you.

5. Don't wear too much jewelry – a few accents are great, whether you prefer delicate or chunkier statement items doesn't matter.

6. Men notice shoes, like heels and strappy styles. High heels make your calves look great and change how you walk. If you can't wear a higher heel, look for a slim, tapered lower heel. And strappy sandals can be very sexy!

My best dating advice is to choose outfits that make you feel fabulous. If you look in the mirror and think to yourself, "Hey, I look good!" then you've done it right. When you feel good about how you look, you actually look better. That's because 80% of your beauty is based on how you feel about yourself.

If you aren't sure what styles and colors look best, consider working with an image consultant or even a friend with style who knows a lot about fashion. I strongly recommend you have at least three go-to dating outfits ready so you don't freak about what to wear when a man asks you out.

Strong Character Presentation

Now let's talk about how you define yourself. Think about who you are and what you have to offer as a mate. Are you easy to get along with and easy to please?

What is your energy level? Do you have a good sense of humor? Do you prefer to be active and get out to do things? Are you a homebody who wants someone to cook for or with and enjoys watching movies?

Knowing who you are and what you want your relationship to be like helps you define how you'll be in a relationship. When you know this, you can share that with the men you meet, painting a picture of what it will be like to spend time with you.

Dating Lesson

Some women feel they need to go to great lengths to attract a man. I'm not saying that at all. I simply want you to be at your very best. No plastic surgery required. This is strictly about making the most of what you've been given. If you want to lose a few pounds or workout with a trainer, go ahead. That doesn't mean you need to wait before you start dating. There's no need to put it off.

Also, please keep your looks in perspective. You want to look good for a first date or singles' event of course. But, I have had clients who pampered all day, got their hair, nails and makeup done, fussed over their clothing and literally prepared for several hours. This can actually be counterproductive.

One client, Sheila, told me after all that preparing all day, she was devastated by an evening where she didn't meet one decent man. She told me flat out she never wanted to go through that again. I agreed with her. She definitely had spent too much time and money on her looks for a simple singles' event. But she wanted to use this disappointment as her reason to stop bothering. Please don't do that to yourself.

Let me tell you what I did when I was out mingling and meeting men. I had six "go-to" outfits that included the following pieces:

- A black jean skirt
- A pair of blue jeans
- A white knit top with ballet neck
- A red "V" neck knit top
- A turquoise "V" neck knit top

That gave me six first-date or man-hunting outfits to choose from. Once this was set, I never struggled again with what to wear. Depending on which items were clean, I had a small dating wardrobe to choose from so I could stop driving myself crazy over the question of what to wear. That was a huge relief and took an enormous amount of the first date jitters out of my preparation. I highly recommend doing this for yourself.

3
Résumé, LinkedIn, Online Dating Profile

Beth - Executive Recruiter & Career Coach

Many people think that the resume gets you the job but the real function of the resume is to get you the interview. A well thought out resume that is eye catching is imperative because in many cases it is the first impression a recruiter or hiring manager will have of you.

As an overview, the resume will consist of several sections, including a career summary, professional experience, education and training, and associations and volunteer activities. Some job seekers may also include publications they have written, certifications and licenses, and other pertinent information.

Considering many recruiters use keyword searches on LinkedIn, etc. to find candidates, it is necessary to have industry or functional acronyms written out as well as using the acronym, i.e., SLA–service level agreement; CPA–Certified Public Accountant.

Avoid these words: responsible, proven track record, references available upon request, hard worker, team player, and detailed oriented. Do a Google search to find more words because others are added to the list every year.

Career Summary

This is the only part of your resume that is not fact but does highlight your key areas and lets your personality come through. It is your interpretation of how you want to portray yourself to others.

For this reason, it is also the hardest part of the resume to write. If the reader is not engaged in reading this section, they most likely will not read the rest of the resume. Considering most resumes only get a six second read, it is crucial to write a catchy piece.

Before the Career Summary, it is a good idea to center a title in bold. It does not have to be a current title but could be more encompassing like Financial Executive or Information Technology Leader. After that, the summary will consist of three to six sentences that showcase your strengths but they also need to be areas you like or want to do more of in the future. As an example, if you don't like to do report writing, don't mention it in your career summary. If you are an amazing leader and mentor then state that (although I would not use the word "amazing").

You may also have bullets underneath to showcase your most prominent attributes or ones that are necessary for a particular field. It is a good idea to also mention any foreign languages skills you may have.

SAMPLE RESUME

Recruiting Specialist & Business Owner

Marketing | Client Management | Candidate Identification

Results driven, innovative, and visionary professional with a record of accomplishment in driving the growth of a 20-year executive search and research business working with clients in a variety of industries and functional areas. Regarded for the ability to successfully develop new business development opportunities with corporate clients and other executive search firms. Recognized as an effective leader, communicator, and business partner who adds value with clients and internal staff. Additional strengths include:

- Effective Negotiation Techniques
- Multi-Tasking/Project Coordination
- New Business Opportunities
- Interpersonal Communications
- Process Improvements
- Strategic Planning & Execution

- Team Collaboration
- Relationship Management

Professional Experience

This section describes in detail your various positions you have held. I suggest to job seekers to go back only 10 to 15 years because you don't want to date yourself. Proper formatting is essential and watch out for typos!

When listing companies make sure that you put the full name of the company, location, and a short blurb about the company that should include sales/revenue size and a description of its products and/or services. Your title should also include the division/business unit name, if applicable. A concise paragraph about your daily responsibilities including staff size you manage comes next. Lastly, have three to five bullets with your key accomplishments and put them in the order from most important to least.

ABC Corporation — Chicago, IL 2007-Present

A leading provider of technology solutions for business, government, and education.

Regional Sales Manager – Greenwich, CT

Supervise 15 salespeople supporting kindergarten through 12th grade (K-12) education business for the Washington, D.C. area. Lead sales training seminars for company nationwide. Interface with vendors, executive management contacts for key accounts, and information technology, and purchasing personnel.

• Create sales strategies to identify lucrative contract opportunities and leverage vendor relationships to achieve significant sales and gain visibility.

• Oversaw major government contract, initially a three-year $200 million program that was extended to five years to upgrade learning for K-12 students throughout the region.

• Identified, negotiated, and executed sizable contracts with Fairfax Educational Services Commission in conjunction with XYZ Corporation.

• Led sales team to be ranked #1 in marketing the product to K-12 classrooms for past four years. Negotiated pricing and leveraged existing contracts to optimize sales.

Education, Training, Certifications, and/or Licenses

The formatting for this section should be consistent with the Professional Experience part. In the previous example, the company was bolded and followed by the location. The same should be applied to a college, training institute, or company issuing a certification or license. Full degree names with majors are listed next. Dates should not be included if it is over 15 years.

Special note: If you are a recent college graduate, you should put your education right after the Career Summary.

Bryant University, Smithfield, RI - Bachelor of Science – Business Administration, cum laude

Baruch College, New York, NY – Master of Business Administration – Marketing Management

College of Executive Coaching, Santa Barbara, CA – Certified Professional Coach

TTI Performance Systems, Ltd., Scottsdale, AZ – Certified Professional Behavioral Analyst – DISC and Certified Professional Motivation Analyst

Associations and Volunteer Activities

This part of the resume is tricky because you want to show that you have other interests, but you also want to avoid someone reading more into it and thus not considering you for the role. I advise clients not to mention religious, political, or children related associations or activities for this reason. Unfortunately, everyone has prejudices and if a recruiter or hiring manager sees that, as an example, you are a Little League coach, it may be assumed you have children and may not be as dedicated to the position as needed.

The best thing is to keep this section to business, industry, and/or functional groups like the Financial Executives Institute, Society of Plastics Engineers, Chambers of Commerce, Rotary clubs, and Women Entrepreneurial Network to name a few.

Other

If you are known for doing speaking engagements, have published articles, conducted special research, and/or hold a patent, that should be mentioned here. It is usually necessary to mention dates here but I would caution that if it is over 15 years old, you may want to mention it instead in the interview and keep it off your resume.

Remember that a resume is your calling card. Spend a lot of time preparing it so that it truly reflects your career and accomplishments. Get others to read it as well and tweak it accordingly.

LinkedIn profile - The big mistake that most people make when they prepare their LinkedIn profile is that they cut and paste their resume and figure they are done. WRONG! LinkedIn is more of a snapshot of you. It still needs to contain pertinent information as detailed above, including keywords but it should not be too long.

Your photo must be a headshot wearing business attire. Using old photos to show that you are young just doesn't work. One financial executive had a photo from the late 1980s (or at least it seemed that way) with big hair and red lips. I told her it reminded me of the Rocky Horror Picture Show. Other pics that will work against you - a man wearing a striped tie with a striped scarf around his neck, Millennials using prom photos, and the real head-scratching photos - a sketch of their face or a photo with their pet or their child. Facebook is not LinkedIn!

Do try to complete every section that LinkedIn will guide you through. You can join 50 groups which helps you expand your network very quickly so I encourage you to do that but do not join social groups unless there is some business reason behind it i.e., you work for a sporting goods or event planning company.

Get recommendations from trusted sources and definitely upload any articles, blogs, videos, or presentations you have done. Use the status line a lot to stay in front of others. You don't necessarily have to post original content but links to articles you may have read that you think others will find interesting. If you are conducting a job search, post "seeking new opportunities" and then be specific on what would be an ideal role for you but don't limit yourself.

LinkedIn is constantly changing its features so keep abreast of new things you can do with your profile. Sometimes they eliminate sections like the reading list so check it frequently.

♥ Ronnie - Dating Coach

Your Online Dating Profile - The Anti-Résumé

While your resume is meant to provide a concise, but complete overview of your career, your online dating profile should be the exact opposite. I recommend my dating coaching clients put the idea of a resume or biography out of their heads. The very last thing you'd ever want to do in a dating profile is give a full overview of your life. That's so boring!

1. The Purpose of Your Online Profile

Let me explain why this is so very different from the resume for job hunting. The purpose of your online dating profile is far less complicated. There is only one purpose and that is to get someone to email you. Yes, that's the whole point. To do that, you don't need all the details. In fact, when people insist on putting every detail in, singles can't be bother reading your lengthy life description. All that work and it will backfire.

What should you include? Well, I'll get to that in a minute, but first, let me tell you the other extremely important distinction between your dating profile and your resume. This is an essential factor that has to do with advertising. The most important thing to remember about advertising is who is reading it. Who is the target audience is the question advertising agencies will ask of their clients. In other words, if you are a single woman, you want to write your profile so it appeals to men.

That might sound silly to you and too simple. Sadly, women make this online dating mistake all the time. They go on and on about all the things they love to do including the ballet, museums, theatre, yoga, etc. These activities will not help you land a man. They could help you attract another woman but I bet that's not what you want. If you want male attention, talking about culture will not help. Most straight men don't care about the ballet.

2. What Men Find Attractive

What do men care about? What do they want to read in your online dating profile? See if any of the options below appeal to you. If they do, talk about them first in your profile. You want to capture a man's attention as fast as possible - then maybe he'll read a bit more and send you an email.

Activities:

- History, particularly American history
- Listening to music – jazz, rock and roll, country
- Playing music, especially drums and guitar of course
- Spectator sports – football, basketball, baseball, soccer, hockey, etc.

- Participative sports – biking, hiking, sailing, kayaking, golfing, skiing, fishing, car racing, etc.

- Additional outdoor activities like camping, etc.

- Current events and the news

Qualities about yourself:

- Easy going
- Easy to get along with
- Easy to please
- Active
- Easy to laugh
- Appreciate men
- Smart
- Outgoing, etc.

Find anything in that list that sounds like you? I sure hope so! Now you know the types of things to write in your profile so men might read it and write to you.

3. Be Positive

When describing yourself and the man you are seeking, don't talk about what you don't want. That will work backwards and cause you to attract it! Instead, focus on what you DO WANT – that works so much better to communicate the kind of guy you are seeking.

Every time you say something like, "No players or couch potatoes," you are admitting you've been taken in by a player and dragged down by a couch potato. That doesn't present you and your relationship choices in a good light. So, keep it positive to make a positive impression.

My client Theresa told men not to contact her if they didn't live within a 50-mile radius or didn't like kids. This made her appear demanding, difficult to please, picky, and unappealing. Yes, you might not want to drive too far, but you don't need to say that upfront. You can just not respond to men who are beyond that distance.

If you have children, at some point the man you are in a relationship with will meet them and need to spend time with them. You are a package deal. But not during the start of dating. This is too much information and overly demanding. Most sites ask if you have children, so you can answer that question without adding more focus on your kids in the profile. Men don't want to date your kids and picturing you as this package eliminates potential romance.

Don't send away prospects by acting like you need to be in that long-term relationship immediately. There is plenty of time later to discuss your children and introduce them if everything is going well with your new man.

4. Optimal Profile Length

Your profile should be three to four short paragraphs. Yes, please break it into paragraphs to make it easier to read. When you have one big block of copy, that is very difficult to read. The total word count should be 300 to 400 words. This will encourage men to take the time to read the profile because it's short. That's another way to appeal to men - brevity.

5. Avoid Sounding Like Everyone Else

You don't need to tell them every facet of your life. What works better is to pick the descriptors about you that will appeal to men. Then say something interesting so you stand out.

If you want to avoid sounding like every other profile on the web, here is my list to avoid:

- Walking on the beach
- Snuggling in front of a fire
- Going to the movies
- Going out to dinner

Everybody likes these activities so you accomplish nothing when you talk about them! None of them will help you stand out.

However, you might argue with me, saying, "I love movies!" Okay, then write about a couple of your favorites and why you like them so much. Now you'll be demonstrating who you are based on your opinions about the movies that touched your soul. This demonstrates your personality rather than making a list of qualities.

6. Words with Double Meaning

I recommend avoiding this list of seven words as they can have a double meaning that can also be read as sexual innuendos. While these descriptors might create a clear picture about you in your mind, don't complain to me if you start to attract "the wrong" kind of men. These words can easily be misinterpreted. The list includes:

- Passionate
- Open-minded
- Adventurous
- Sensual
- Casual
- Daring
- I'll try anything once

7. Be Honest

On a resume, sometimes you drop off the oldest job to appear younger. This is a little smoke and mirrors and is relatively harmless. In your profile however, I recommend being honest about your age. People will find out anyway and then they might wonder what else you lied about. Don't risk this deal breaker.

If you want to be found in a particular age bracket, then fudge your age a little when you fill out the online form. You can come clean at the end of your profile. Say something like, "I'm really 41, but didn't want to be excluded from the 30-40 searches." This way you'll be included in the search, but clear up the age thing immediately with the truth in your profile. Then you can avoid those awkward conversations later when you have to admit how old you really are and that you lied.

Lastly, fudging a few pounds is better than a lot of years. If you want to shave off 2 - 3 years, what the heck. But if you try lying about 5 - 10 years or more because you think you really look young, this won't go over well when the man you're dating does find out. Please don't do it. You are who you are - admit it and be proud of it.

When I was dating, I met a guy who was younger than I was, but I didn't know by how much. After four or five dates, he had his driver's license out of his wallet and I grabbed it to look at his picture. Next thing I noticed was his birthday. He was seven years younger than I was, but had admitted only to four. I asked why he did that and he said he thought I wouldn't date him. But it did cause me to have doubts about him. Don't spoil your chances with lies, even little white lies.

8. Avoid Lists and Use Descriptive Words

Lists are boring! It's a yawner when you read a profile with a long list of adjectives separated by commas. Instead, you want to demonstrate your qualities.

For example, instead of saying "I'm creative and have a good sense of humor" you could say, "I love to cook and make up my own recipes. Most times my creations are delicious. Once in awhile I mess up and end up ordering take out." That's funny; it shows your creativity, and your ability to laugh at yourself – all good qualities!

Also, use Thesaurus.com to pick out juicy words that are more descriptive than what might come to mind naturally. I'm not talking about using those 25-cent words to look smart. Juicy, descriptive words make a profile fun to read! For example, "I love when the sky is the fresh, icy blue that reminds me of icebergs." You get the idea.

9. Photo Do's and Dont's

This is a must! Please use current photos or not more than three years old. There is nothing more disappointing for a person meeting you then when you look nothing like your picture. Don't play this silly game. The men will see you soon enough and know you have aged, gained weight, or cut your hair. Own your looks and be proud of who you are today. Make the most of what you have. Yes, I know men do this too, but that doesn't mean it works for them either.

Professional photos can really help. A good photographer knows about lighting and can bring out your best features and capture your smile. Photographers know how to deal with the background as well and make the whole photo presentation look good.

If you are going to take your own pictures, think about what is behind you. You don't want laundry hanging over the banister. Yes, my clients have done this! Avoid showing your messy house. Clean up one area so the entire picture is pleasing and make sure there is nothing distracting behind you.

A few other tips for good photos:

- Stand up – you always look thinner
- Tuck your chin just a little so you don't appear arrogant
- Don't wear sunglasses – everybody wants to see your eyes
- Wear solid colored clothing rather than busy patterns, stripes or prints
- Men like red and pink so if you have a good outfit – wear it!
- Make the most of your figure
- Wear a date-worthy outfit
- Do your hair and makeup

Remember, the point of your profile is to get someone to email you. So don't go overboard in length and detail. And most importantly, post it so you can start meeting men!

Dating Lesson

There are so many do's and dont's for online dating I can't get to them all in this one chapter. The amount of tips I could share would be a book all by itself! However, I want to be sure you are aware of the biggest pitfalls so you can avoid them more easily.

• Don't fall in love with a profile. It's just words. You must meet a man to know if he could be a good match.

• Don't fall for the virtual relationship with texts, emails, or calls. This is not dating or true love, no matter what he tells you. Real love involves face-to-face dates. How else can you kiss and determine chemistry? Don't fall for these guys who reel you in with sweet daily texts, but don't have time to see you in person. No excuses!

• Don't get upset reading profiles when you see what some men want in a woman. Just move on and stop worrying about those men.

• Don't get upset if the "wrong men" contact you. Simply delete their emails and move on to stay positive.

• Don't respond to every man, especially if you aren't interested. It's not rude to not respond- it's actually appropriate and less hurtful.

• Know that only 10 - 20% of men will respond to your emails and that is perfectly normal. Expect a low response rate so you aren't bent out of shape or disappointed.

• Don't get prematurely attached to a man who seems good "on screen." The point of online dating is to get your dating journey started by meeting new people.

• Don't get invested in the computer matching and algorithm stuff. You still have to do all the screening work because a software program cannot determine chemistry or find you love.

Here are a few important things to do as well:

• Do get used to meeting new people and let it build your confidence and skills.

• Do date more than one man at a time until you are exclusive.

• Do date different types of men, not just your "type" to find your best match.

• Do give it some time to work out. Match.com suggests a year not because of the money, but because they know you might need to kiss a few frogs before you connect with the right guy.

- Do find a way to enjoy the process because finding love takes time. If you have a bad date, turn it into a funny story to share with friends and laugh about it.

Cover Letter

Beth - Executive Recruiter & Career Coach

The interesting thing about a cover letter is that it is protocol to prepare and submit a cover letter for most positions but many recruiters and hiring managers will admit that they never read them (including me!). Considering most of your resume is a list of facts about you coupled with a career summary that highlights key areas, the cover letter is the only marketing document where you can really promote yourself and explain why you are an ideal candidate to work for that organization.

Some companies do require that a cover letter should be submitted with the resume. There usually are key areas that the hiring organization wants you to include in the cover letter such as how you learned of the position (if applicable), critical skills that you must possess, salary requirements, and relocation considerations. Some industries or organizations, like government agencies and universities, expect very lengthy and detailed letters describing accomplishments, but more importantly how one's expertise would fit the qualifications of the role.

The header of the cover letter should be the same as it is for the resume. Font size, type and color, if used, should be exactly the same. The full name of the person with a Mr. or Ms. in front of it is required. The next line should contain the person's EXACT title that may include an officer title and a functional title like Senior Vice President and Chief Financial Officer. The address should be complete as if you are addressing an envelope. Even if you are emailing the cover letter, a full address should be listed. To the right, there should be a date for when the letter was sent. The person should be addressed "Dear Mr. Last Name." Unless you have spoken with the person, do not use the first name in the salutation section.

For a standard cover letter, I suggest three paragraphs that are concise and utilize industry and/or job specification words. However, do not use words that are superfluous. The first paragraph should explain the reason for contacting this company or organization. Some reasons could be that you were referred; you saw an advertisement; you like their products or services; you heard they had a good reputation; and/or you read an article about the company.

The next paragraph explains what qualities and experience you could bring to a particular role or if you are sending your resume unsolicited, highlight your attributes you feel the company would view as an asset. In other words, describe your value proposition. Do not tell them what areas you may be light in or do not have experience in i.e., "I am well versed in Excel but only have some knowledge of PowerPoint." The key thing to remember here is "what is in it for them?" "What is it about your background they feel would benefit their organization?"

In today's world, companies are moving very quickly and are still very cost conscious. Although they provide training to their employees, most employers want employees who can "hit the ground running." If you are looking to change industries or functions, this second paragraph not only needs to articulate how your skills and expertise are transferrable but also needs to explain how you can bring fresh ideas and strategies that will benefit the company.

The last paragraph is boilerplate. It explains that the resume is attached for review. It also states that you will follow up in a week's time (if appropriate) and that if additional information is needed to contact you and again provide your phone number. The last line should be a positive closing statement like "I look forward to speaking with you soon."

Do not sound desperate and/or meek. "I really hope you find my resume interesting" or "I really want you to call me." It is expected you are trying to promote yourself but do not be so bold and boastful. Other things that turn potential employers off include:

• Negativity - do not badmouth your current boss, company, or the duties of your job. It is correct to say that "you are ready for a more challenging role" but not "I am so bored and my boss is a jerk."

• Lifestyle - do not mention that you are interested in a position because it fits your lifestyle. "I can ride my bike to work so I can save money on gas"; "I have small children so I know you will give me flex hours or I can work from home when I need to"; or "I like that you have a picnic table outside so I can eat my lunch there." It is acceptable to state that the mission of the company fits your values or your life as in "I am an avid sportsman and have used your company's protein products for years."

• Spelling errors and/or poor grammar - you only have one opportunity to contact this person so do not make any mistakes.

• Economy - although the poor economy affected many people, do not bring it up in your cover letter. You will be perceived as disgruntled and whiny. In your first paragraph you can mention that your position was eliminated due to a downsizing or a company move but do not sound like a complainer. You can also add that during this time you have learned new skills, etc.

Cover Letter Template

Header (should replicate resume header)

Mr./Ms. Name

Street address

City, State Zip

Date

Dear Mr./Ms. Name:

I read with interest in (name of publication) regarding (name of position) with your company.

I recently read an article or saw an advertisement...

I was referred to your company by...

Second sentence and on - I regard (company name's) reputation because I desire to work in a progressive and admired organization. Throughout my career, I have demonstrated strong hospitality management expertise working with hotels, restaurants, and franchised establishments. As I pursue new opportunities, I would be pleased to leverage these, and my other skills, which include my effective marketing, sales, and training capability.

Recently I served as Operations Manager for XXX Company. In this role, I oversaw 120 restaurants with revenues of over $400 million. A representative sample of the value I offer:

§ Interacted heavily with franchisees to open new retail locations and to introduce new product offerings and marketing campaigns resulting in increased sales.

§ Served as General Manager for a hotel in Germany and conceived, developed, and launched two restaurants in Manhattan.

§ Led innovative sales and marketing initiatives to successfully launch point of sales system to international restaurant chains.

Please find attached my resume for your perusal. I would welcome the opportunity to review my credentials with you in an interview. Please contact me at phone number to arrange a convenient time to speak.

—OR—

Please find attached my resume for your review. I will follow up with you in a week's time. In the meantime, if you need additional information, please contact me at phone #. I look forward to speaking with you soon.

Regards,

Full name

Enclosure: Résumé

E. Elizabeth "Beth" Carter
Street address | town, state zip code | cell # | email

Sara Smith
Director – Career Services
ABC Company
1150 High Street
Fairfield, CT 06824

May 5, 2014

Dear Sara:

It was a pleasure to speak with you today regarding the Manager – Employee Development position at ABC Company. Throughout my career, I have demonstrated strong expertise in identifying and marketing my firms' executive search, research, and business and executive coaching services to a wide variety of clients, including small businesses and Fortune 500 companies. I strongly feel this position would utilize all of my skills and more importantly, my contacts within the business community, associations, and the Bryant alumni network.

Currently, I am the owner of two businesses – Carter Consultants Ltd., a research and executive search firm, and Beth Carter Enterprise, a newly formed business, executive, and career coaching company. The following is a representative sample of the value I offer:

- Serve as a business partner with clients in developing recruiting strategies to hire and retain middle and senior level individuals in such areas as manufacturing, human resources, legal, general management, retail, and marketing.

- Provide guidance as a "thought partner" for corporate leaders, business owners, and those in career transition.

- Develop new business development opportunities with corporate clients and other executive search firms.

Please find attached my resume for your review. I look forward to meeting with you and your staff at 9:00 a.m. on Friday, June 13. If you have any questions and/or need additional information in the interim, please call me at cell #. I am very interested in this exciting opportunity.

Sincerely,

E. Elizabeth Carter

Enclosure: Résumé

4
Elevator Speech: Presenting Yourself

Beth - Executive Recruiter & Career Coach

When you are at a networking event, how do you introduce yourself? You are in the grocery store and you run into a friend you haven't seen in awhile and you want to tell them you are conducting a job search; what do you say? The 30 or 60-second pitch, also known as the elevator speech, is one of the most difficult parts of the job search. You have a brief period of time to convey to the other person who you are in terms of skills and qualifications and what you are seeking in a new opportunity. In other words, it is taking all your work experiences and knowledge and truncating it into a two or three-sentence statement.

I tell my clients that it is their Nike swoosh; it is their commercial that they are broadcasting to others. The hard part is that not only does it require all the essential elements, but it also has to be creative and thought provoking so the audience remembers and more importantly acts on it. You want people to tell others about you! Just make sure the statement is accurate.

In addition, the delivery of the elevator speech is just as important as the content. I can't tell you how many times I have been at career transition workshops where people stand up, look insecure or bored and mumble their words. They also may appear to not have any energy and/or come across as not wanting to talk about themselves. In reality, not many people want to share their elevator speech, but it is your calling card and you need to say it with confidence so others realize you have a lot to offer a new employer.

Before you develop your elevator speech, you need to take a good look at yourself. Do you excel in giving presentations and speeches? Do you enjoy and feel comfortable getting up in front of people? If not, you should consider working with a public speaking coach. These are experts who work with individuals to make their presentations more effective and meaningful. They help their clients overcome their fears and insecurities. Most importantly, they assist their clients in finding their authentic self and portraying it well to others.

If you still feel anxious, then practice your commercial in front of a mirror. Watch for good eye contact. Notice body language signals that could be seen as negative. As an example, I had a client who talked to others with her arms crossed. Although she was a warm and engaging person when she was with people she knew well, she received feedback from her coworkers that was perceived as hard to please and always looked a bit annoyed. The solution we came up for her was for her to carry a pen around so that she would think twice before she crossed her arms.

Here are the steps in preparing your elevator speech:

1. Select a few words that describe you well. This is a similar exercise when you are writing the career summary of your resume. The difference is that words need to be functionally or industry specific in your pitch versus adjectives that describe your overall persona. So instead of saying "diligent, resourceful, and innovative marketing professional" which would be correct for your resume, your commercial should start off like this: "I am a marketing, branding, and advertising senior manager or I excel at …"

2. The next phrase should discuss the industry experience you have and/or want to pursue. You can be generic here by saying financial services, but it would be more helpful to your audience to say investment management or insurance or commercial banking. It is also acceptable to say that you want to transition from one industry to another, but you may need more of an explanation here. "My expertise has been in the mailing systems business calling on government agencies. My sales skills would also work well in the medical equipment field because I would be calling on the same customers I am looking to transition into this industry."

Don't be concerned if some people don't understand your field. They probably can't give you referrals anyway; however, you may be nicely surprised. Be sure the ones who can assist you truly understand what you are looking for in your next position.

3. Finally, you want to have a statement that makes an impression on your listeners. That is the most difficult part because not only does it have to be memorable, it also has to be associated with you.

There was a Wendy's advertisement with the tagline "Where's the Beef?" Many people had seen the ad, but most people could not remember if it was an ad for Wendy's, Burger King, or McDonald's. The point is you want your listener to understand your message, be able to successfully remember it, and market you to others.

4. After you have it all written down, take a red pen and cross off any words that are redundant or boring or not critical to your speech. Keep in mind that when people listen to you, they are thinking, "what is in it for me?" Once you realize this, not only will your elevator pitch be great, but also it will affect the way you conduct your whole search strategy.

Here are some other tips:

• Be honest - It is important to market yourself but some people get carried away and embellish their elevator speech. This is unethical and most of the people you speak to are bright and can spot a phony pretty easily.

• Keep it short - As stated before, keep your elevator speech to 2-3 sentences. Pretend you are in an elevator with someone and that is the amount of time you have to sell yourself; this is usually about a minute. If you talk more than that, you will come across as rambling which will turn your listener off.

• Practice, practice, practice - Rehearse in front of a mirror, and/or pitch your elevator speech to a business colleague, family member, or friend. Ask them to recite what they heard back to you to ensure that the message you are trying to convey is accurate. Make edits to your speech and practice it again.

• Don't memorize it verbatim - You may forget something and then you will panic. Instead be comfortable with what you are saying and don't force it.

• Pay attention to your body language - Look at the way you position your body especially your arm movements. Having your arms by your side is acceptable but don't look stiff. Be careful with such actions; I had a client who twirled her hair around her finger and when I pointed it out, she had not even realized she was doing it. People react as much to nonverbal cues as they do to what you are saying. It would be advantageous to video record your speech so you can see for yourself what you look like to others. Don't forget to smile!

The most successful people making elevator speeches look poised, confident, and genuine. A succinct and memorable commercial will inspire others to help you succeed in finding that next great opportunity. Here is an example...

"Hello. My name is Batman. I excel at fighting crime and putting bad guys in jail. With my trusty partner, Robin, I am adept at working with law enforcement officers to make Gotham City a safer place to live. In my next role, I want to manage a larger team and work to combat larger crime rings."

♥ Ronnie - Dating Coach

What to Say about Yourself at a Singles Event

Whether you are seeking a new job or looking for new business, you have a rehearsed pitch that gives the new people you meet a snapshot about who you are. Why not do the same thing for a singles' event or when you first meet someone socially? Can you think of what you could say?

I recommend my dating coaching clients prepare something to say for several reasons. First, it can help a lot if you are the type who gets nervous meeting new people. Having a couple of sentences ready keeps you from worrying about what to say. Second, if you practice, you can come across as confident about who you are and this is just as important for dating as it is for job hunting. Both genders are attracted to confident people and seek this quality in a mate.

Now, I don't want you to think this is supposed to sound canned or rehearsed. The idea is to know what you want to say, not repeat it word for word, exactly the same way every time. That probably won't feel natural in a social situation. However, knowing generally what to say when someone asks, "Tell me about yourself" can go a long way to help people know who you are and make you feel more comfortable with that question.

What should you say? That all depends on how you want to portray yourself. Here are some things you can string together to give the people a quick idea of who you are. You don't need to rattle everything off all at once, but keep these suggestions in your "back pocket" when you are asked a question.

1. What town are you from?

2. Where did you grow up?

3. What kind of work do you do? (not where, that's a private detail)

4. What are two-three fun activities you enjoy?

5. What's your favorite movie or top three? Why do you like them?

6. What TV shows do you watch?

7. What kind of music do you listen to?

8. What sports do you follow?

9. Where did you go to college and what did you like about it?

10. Do you have a passion in life?

11. What do you do in your free time?

12. What do you do on a beautiful Sunday afternoon?

13. What do you do on a rainy Sunday?

14. What type of exercise do you prefer?

15. What's your favorite cuisine?

Even if this sounds silly, this exercise actually helps you get reacquainted with yourself. Many midlife singles have forgotten what makes them unique or interesting to a potential suitor. As many people go through the motions of their day, they sometimes lose touch with the different aspects of their life because they are simply too close to it.

Another huge benefit of taking time to work this through is that you are actually coming up with conversation starters. On a first date, you may have a list of questions in mind to qualify a date for the future. If you are going to ask a string of questions, you had better have your own answers figured out for those same questions. And, you will never be at a loss for what to talk about with these 15 topics.

Now, I want you to pay attention to what is not on the list. Nothing about your children, your ex, your health, finances, divorce, or dating. No complaints of any kind. The point is to focus on you and what makes you a fun person to spend time with. You can mention you're a mom, but don't spend a lot of time on this, especially when you first meet a man.

Let's look at an example of how preparing a description of yourself can work for you by seeing how I did this with one of my dating coaching clients, Caroline.

Caroline is 44 and divorced for three years. She has two kids in school and works as a nurse at the local hospital. She enjoys baseball, listens to country and rock and roll music, and loves Zumba and yoga to stay fit. Every chance she gets, she spends time outdoors and in nature. Caroline is a big movie fan and likes chick flicks, thrillers, and action films. She adores Thai food and other Asian cuisines and grew up in the same town she lives in currently.

Here's what Caroline could say about herself as a brief introduction when someone says, "Tell me about yourself":

"I grew up in Fairfield and still live here because I love it. I tend to spend a lot of my free time outdoors in nature. Country music is really fun, but I also enjoy classic 70s rock and roll like the Eagles. And I love the movies – every weekend I find a new film to watch."

You not only say what you spend time doing, but add energy by saying what you like about it. She mentioned four things about herself but it added up to only three sentences – so it's quick. This kind of overview helps your date by giving him the opportunity to learn about you and ask you questions.

Caroline's conversation partner could ask her about the town she lives in, growing up and schools, a new movie that just came out, country music, her favorite Eagles album, and more. There's lots to talk about which is the whole point!

If you are having difficulty thinking about yourself this way, here are some questions to consider. You might like both items in a set so that's OK too. The point is to remember who you are, get to know yourself again and come up with things to talk about when you first meet people or on the first couple of dates.

- Jazz or Rock and Roll?

- Coke or Pepsi?

- Cats or dogs?

- Jeans or little black dress?

- Nature or culture?

- Camping or Holiday Inn?

- Chocolate or fruit?

- Coffee or tea?

- News or comedy?

- Novels or nonfiction?

- Hockey or basketball?

- Team sports or individual sports (tennis etc.)?

- Vacations or weekend trips?

- Foreign or U.S. travel?

- Skiing or beaching?

- Type A personality or easy going?

Invest a little time thinking about these ideas and you will be so happy you did next time you're at a singles event and have to make conversation! My clients are always pleasantly surprised with how much this exercise helps them feel more comfortable in those naturally awkward moments when you start talking to someone new.

Dating Lesson

Your elevator speech and how you talk about yourself in a dating situation has to sound genuine which is not easy if you tend to get nervous. Some people feel awkward talking about themselves or just talking with someone new.

Here are a few tips to handle nervousness:

• If you perspire when you get nervous, wear a dark top or blazer. Then you won't let them see you "sweat" and I mean that literally.

• Strengthen your self-esteem by wearing something really pretty that makes you feel great. This helps so much when you encounter rejection. At the very least, you know you looked good!

• To appear confident, practice what you are going to say. Just like you wouldn't go to an interview without rehearsing what you want to say, the same applies for this kind of socializing. This is particularly true if you aren't used to talking about yourself. Try talking in front of a mirror and make sure that you smile, relax your shoulders, and believe what you are saying.

• If you have been known to stretch the truth due to nerves, push yourself to be more accurate. Add a little "color" to your story if you feel like it, but keep in mind the truth is far easier to remember.

• Avoid pretentious words so you don't trip over them or suddenly feel tongue-tied.

• No need to impress – just be yourself because you can easily keep that up.

• If you speak too quickly, try to calm yourself and speak slowly. Take a breath and pause occasionally. The pause is very effective because it allows the other person to take a moment to digest what you are saying and the opportunity to respond.

• In addition to smiling, laughter can work wonders to break the tension. Keep in mind that on a first date, the man you're meeting is probably as nervous as you are, if not more. By making a joke or telling a funny story, it allows you to share a laugh. The vast majority of women tell me they want a man with a sense of humor so this is a good trial run.

• You can simply admit to your date you feel nervous. Say something like, "I am a bit nervous" or "I have been looking forward to meeting you but now I'm nervous." Being honest upfront can set a solid foundation for what might turn into a long-lasting and true relationship.

This is a good lesson on why you need to be yourself and not try to be anyone else. I had a client, Barbara, who pretended to be the woman she thought men would like. After six months dating a guy she really liked, she told me she couldn't keep up the façade anymore. She decided to revert to being herself. It was a shame because the man she was dating didn't know who the real Barbara was. As a result, he freaked out at the change in her and broke things off. Be yourself; just be your best self.

I had another client, a man named Greg who was always very nervous when he met someone new. The same thing always happened when he didn't know what to say. He would start to compliment the woman. While that seems like it could be a good thing, he didn't stop at one or two compliments. He'd tell her she was beautiful, then he liked her hair. She had nice shoes; she seemed really smart, etc. This sounded insincere to women and they were turned off fast.

We worked together to help him craft some simple conversation starters and that changed everything for Greg. I share this with you so that you know men often get nervous on a first date too. Be sure to allow for this and give men a chance.

5
Multiple Search Approach: Career & Dating

Beth - Executive Recruiter & Career Coach

Many people do not like the term "networking" because it sounds like work. It's better to view this task as "personal growth" which has a more positive connotation. Networking to meet new people expands your world and your options as you connect with others in the workforce.

For your job search, this perspective makes a tremendous difference. When you think of the goal as learning from every person you encounter instead of simply meeting x number of people in a set period of time, you are more likely to have an uplifting and rewarding experience.

As a recruiter, I recommend a five-prong approach to my clients rather than relying on one or two ways to meet so you can avoid putting all your eggs in one basket. The more methods used to build your network and inform your contacts, the better your chances for finding employment.

The Five-Prong Networking Approach

1. Contact Personal Network. Once a resume is created, the job seeker should immediately email resumes to everyone in his or her personal network. This includes people known locally and nationwide - family, friends, former co-workers, past bosses, neighbors, college classmates, and association members. Simply email a copy to yourself and blind copy everyone else with a short note like this:

"I have recently started conducting a job search, seeking _____ position to utilize my skills and learn new ones. I am interested in staying in the _____ area (or are open to relocation). I also want to continue to manage/become a manager/be a sole contributor. [List one more desire.]

Please find my resume attached for your review. If you can assist me by forwarding my resume to others or by providing any leads, I would greatly appreciate it. For additional information, please contact me at _____. Thank you for your assistance."

DO NOT write this, which one of my clients did:

"Hey dudes! I got laid off in March and am looking for a new job. As you know, I prefer riding my motorcycle to work so I must work at a place that has a covered garage. My last boss was a jerk (probably because she was a woman) so I think a guy boss would be better for me. Attached is my resume. Thanks for your help."

2. Review Job Boards. The second approach is to review the job boards such as Indeed.com, Craigslist, and specialty niche recruiting websites for particular industries and functional areas. These sites are useful for three reasons -

- They showcase jobs you can apply for.

- They use "buzz words" you can use for your resume, cover letter, and interview.

- They help you identify recruiters specializing in your area.

In addition, I recommend you conduct a search using the word "sales" to determine which companies are hiring multiple salespeople. An organization recruiting several sales people is positioning itself for growth and is likely proactive vs. reactive. They will need additional staff people to support the expansion, which is a tip off to where more jobs could be opening.

3. Work with Recruiters - Recruiters are an essential part of the job search process, however, you need to understand that there are two types of recruiters. Contingency recruiters work solely on commission (like a real estate agent) and tend to conduct lower level searches or in niche markets like insurance or medical sales. Retained recruiters are hired by companies to investigate a particular industry or functional area and present only the best candidates.

The search process with retained recruiters tends to take longer and is primarily used for management and executive level positions. Keep in mind all recruiters are compensated by the hiring companies and that is where their loyalties reside. By all means, submit your resume for their databases, but don't think they will "market" or guide you which is a big misconception many have about recruiters.

4. Leverage Social Media - Since 2008, the use of LinkedIn in particular, has become a key piece of the job search. Candidates without a profile or at least a skeleton of one are frowned upon by recruiters and hiring managers. A well thought out and eye catching "profile" is the equivalent of the 30 second commercial used during networking which makes key words and positioning essential.

Don't just repeat your resume on LinkedIn. Instead, highlight specific areas that will entice recruiters to contact you for additional information and your resume. To become more visible, become an active member by joining groups, posting articles or other points of interest, and connecting with people. The more active you are, the more people will see you as an expert in your field, and will want to refer you and possibly hire you!

On the flip side, be careful what you post on other social media sites like Facebook and Twitter. Both recruiters and hiring managers often check your profile to see what they can learn about your life, so think twice about what you post during a job search. Photos that include drinking, drugs, guns, and nudity are not acceptable at all! One client who hunts tried to explain this to me but I still told him to remove the photo immediately.

5. Take the Direct Approach - The most challenging part of networking is using the direct approach. Start by developing a list of companies that you are interested in and then contact them directly. Review Chapter 3 and write a cover letter with your reasons for wanting to join them and include your resume. Send it to the hiring manager and do NOT send correspondence to the human resources department or to "whom it may concern" because both options will likely not get the attention you desire.

In the last paragraph of the cover letter, mention how you will be following up with the recipient in a week's time. This demonstrates that you are a proactive job seeker who knows your value and sees yourself as an asset. It also tells a company that you have done "your homework" and know who the decision makers are in the organization.

By combining these five approaches simultaneously, you will be seen as someone who knows what they want and are not afraid to go after it. You will get more interviews which will help to refine your interviewing skills and build confidence. The more interviews, the better your chances of receiving multiple offers and landing a job which is a powerful position to be in.

♥ Ronnie - Dating Coach

Beth's suggestions about the multiple search approach completely align with my dating strategy. I encourage my clients to think of dating as an opportunity to meet new people. First and foremost, take the pressure off. When you approach each date this way, you can stop worrying if every new man you meet is "the one."

As you go on more and more first dates, you'll build skills and confidence too; the same as with job hunting. The more people you meet and know, the better your chances of finding a job or a romantic partner! I'm in sync with Beth's plan and have my own version of the five-prong approach applied to dating.

5 Part Approach to Dating

1. Ask for Fix Ups - As a dating coach since 2002 combined with my own personal dating experience, one thing I know for sure is that blind dates lead to love! This is how I met my husband. Contacting your personal network to tell them you are looking for love and asking for help can be highly effective. Statistics show that 30% of couples met through other people.

When I started my journey to find love, I only asked the people I knew and really trusted. I wanted to be comfortable talking about dating. But with time and practice, I started discussing my search with the new people I met as well.

Here's my story. One night I met my friend Carol, at a local bar and she invited several other women to join us. I was angry because you can't meet men when you are hanging around with a bunch of women. I decided to just go with it and pushed myself to relax and start getting to know them.

I got into a great conversation with a woman named Maureen who, after 30-minutes, asked me if I was seeing anyone. She thought her brother Paul would like me. He was my last first date and she was right - he did like me. Yes, I married her brother! Thank you Maureen.

Do not underestimate the power of your personal contacts and network which includes friends, family, neighbors, colleagues, fellow volunteers, and anyone you come in contact with who seems like they know a lot of people. Go for it!

Fix ups and blind dates work and so does networking. I know a woman who went to a networking meeting with love in mind. When it was her turn to talk about the kind of business clients she was looking for, she was bold and said something completely unexpected. She said she wanted to find love and asked if anyone knew a single guy she could meet.

Yes, Molly asked all those business people to fix her up and help her find love. And she did! A local real estate agent liked her bravado and thought his brother might like her too. He had been divorced a while and wasn't meeting many woman. Josh fixed Molly up with his brother and they've been married about 8 years.

Keep in mind the same principles apply as in business networking. Most people know approximately 250 people. That means if you ask 25 people for help, that gives you access to approximately 6,250 people. The more people in your network, the better your chances of finding a good match.

2. Try Online Dating - Just like with a job search, it's easier to go where the jobs are listed. For dating, it's easier to find singles where they gather and the biggest place is online. As men age, they tend to be less social, so they go to fewer events and become less visible. Where do they spend time? Online!

In the past, online dating was seen as something people tried when they grew desperate. Today, with 40-50 million people using these sites in the U.S. alone, it has become a mainstream method to meet singles. The stigma is gone and online dating is the fastest and cheapest way to jumpstart your love life.

Other places you can meet singles are in singles groups like Parents without Partners. You can find many singles social clubs and groups on www.Meetup.com including singles dances, group activities like kayaking, hiking, biking, and even gourmet clubs.

Dating is a numbers game. The more people you meet, the more opportunities to find the right match for you.

3. Hire a Matchmaker - Depending on your age and where you live, hiring a matchmaker, which is like an employment recruiter but for dating, can be another viable option to help you meet men. However, you cannot rely on this method alone because you will not meet enough people. It may take some time to find guys who meet your criteria. In the meantime, you can try some of the other options so you are not stagnant and waiting on them.

One thing to keep in mind about matchmakers and dating services is that most have a 30/70 ratio of men to women. That's great if you're a man, but stinks as a woman. Sometimes the ratio is a little higher, maybe 40/60 and things can be better in a large city. Many of my dating coaching clients over 40 complain bitterly about these services because often matchmakers just don't have the inventory needed over 40 or 50.

Remember, a matchmaker can only fix you up with the men they have in their databases. It's not like they go out and specifically seek the guy you described. That would be nice but it doesn't work that way. Maybe it does for one of those millionaire-dating services, but then you could be paying $10,000 - $50,000. Oh and most people are not millionaires.

If you are a woman in her 20s or 30s who doesn't mind dating older men, matchmakers and dating services could be a good addition to your other ways of meeting new people. But it does come with a price tag that's usually a couple of thousands of dollars. And there are no guarantees.

4. Leverage Social Media - Yes, social media can help you connect with potential dates too! Facebook is involved in more and more romantic partners as people look through their friends' friends to find prospects. If you see someone in your friend's newsfeed that catches your eye, ask to be introduced or reach out yourself when he makes a comment that inspires you.

Friends online can turn into live dates as long as you move to meet face-to-face. Don't get lost in online or texting chats for months at a time which can easily happen. You might start to believe you have a relationship developing, but the cold truth is this leads nowhere and will keep you single. Don't fall into this trap too as so many women do, thinking all that virtual communication has meaning or that the man is into you. If he was into you, he'd want to see you for live dates no matter how busy he is.

5. Take the Direct Approach - You can actually meet men anywhere you go once you wake up and realize that single men are literally everywhere. Learn how to turn on the feminine charm, flirt, and strike up a conversation. Once you do, you can meet men in line at the bank, grocery store, or cleaners. You might be buying new sheets, buying a book, or getting a cup of coffee. Probably 98% of men would be happy to have a woman chat with them and will find it quite flattering.

Places where you are likely to meet men so you can try the direct approach include:

• Starbucks

• Barnes and Noble (especially near the café or magazine section)

• Dog parks (so walk your dog there if you have one)

• Whole Foods near the prepared foods

• In a deli or sandwich shop that has a good take out business at lunch time

• Wal-Mart – a recent study showed more people found love at first site at this big box retailer than anywhere else!

Getting comfortable being flirty and friendly will take some practice and gumption. But it's totally worth it! Flirting with men is not sleazy. It's about being friendly, open, and approachable. You are making it easier for men to connect with you, so don't worry.

Being friendly isn't the same as teasing some guy. There are no "promises" with flirting—it's just good fun.

And the best part? There is often more than one man at a time who notices you. When you are friendly to one guy, it can encourage others to take the chance of approaching you too. They can see you are engaging and won't be mean or rude if they take the risk to talk with you. Make sure you are nice to men in public – you never know who else is watching!

Dating Lesson

When you are looking for a new job, do you explore only one option at a time? I hope not! If you are serious about finding new employment, you want to maximize your options to land the best assignment. The same holds true for dating. Trouble is, most women meet a man and rather than continuing to date, they want to see what happens with that one guy.

This is a HUGE dating mistake. The last thing you want to do is narrow your options before you get to exclusivity with a man. Why is that? Because you don't know if he'll work out or call again. He may be just dating around, not looking for a relationship or not your cup of tea. It takes time to get to know a man to see if he has true Mr. Right potential. You can't know when he might fizzle out and disappear, so don't put all your eggs in one basket prematurely.

The best thing you can do is hedge your bets and keep your options open. That's why I recommend dating more than one man at a time. I'm not talking about being in a relationship with more than one man so don't get confused. Dating is the process of determining if you want to invest more time with a person. You are collecting data and observing behavior to discover if you are a good fit and if he is the one for you.

Heartbreak occurs when you go on a couple of dates with a guy you like and then decide to drop your other options or don't continue to look for additional suitors. You allow yourself to get emotionally invested in a man before you know if he is the right one. Then he disappears or you have a disagreement and you have to start all over again. Plus, you feel let down because you had your heart set on a guy you didn't really know.

Don't make this dating mistake as so many women do. Continue to date any man who asks and who seems like he has potential until you discuss exclusivity. That is the time to drop other guys and focus on the one who is showing you he's serious about a relationship. Do not close off your options even one minute before exclusivity is discussed. And don't skip the conversation and just assume you are the only woman a man is dating.

When you relax and take the pressure off, you can end up meeting and dating more men. That helps you find a good match. See if you can learn to simply enjoy meeting new people. This improves your confidence and makes you that much more appealing. You'll realize that if this guy doesn't work out, there are plenty more. You won't be as hard hit by rejection or disappointment when a man doesn't ask you out again.

Last but not least, you won't need a long time to recover from making the mistake of narrowing your options too quickly and focusing on the wrong man. The longer you keep things light versus serious, the more objective you can remain. Keep your eyes open to make sure you are qualifying the men you date. That's the best way to avoid ending up with the wrong man; take your time getting to know him first before becoming exclusive.

6
Phone Interviews & First Phone Calls

Beth - Executive Recruiter & Career Coach

Phone interviews are becoming more common in the recruiting process. If there is more than one, the first is usually with a recruiter, followed by the hiring manager. Many candidates overlook preparing much for this type of interview which is a big mistake. They assume because the interview is not face-to-face that they can wing it. Preparation is just as important if not more so with a phone interview.

These are my suggestions for making a good impression during your phone interviews.

• Before the interview, conduct extensive research to find out about the person you will be interviewing with as well as company history, financials, marketing, and any other pertinent data. Keep your notes in front of you to refer to during the conversation. In addition, have your resume handy and a paper and pen to take notes.

• Use a landline if possible and disable phone features like call waiting. A landline provides better call quality and eliminates the possibility of dropped calls. Choose a quiet place for the conversation. If you are speaking at home, make sure your children are in another room, and the landscaper and or cleaning lady are not scheduled for that day and no dogs barking in the background. Close the windows too.

• Be honest but not too honest. Recruiters understand that things happen especially when the candidate is talking from a residence. It could be cats fighting outside your door, a glass is knocked over, or a spouse interrupts your call. However, don't do what one candidate did to me. She admitted that she was not prepared for our call because she had been mopping her floor. Another one was outside to take the call so that she could walk around her yard while she was talking to me. Needless to say, they left a bad impression with me.

• Dress for the part. Too often people take a casual tone on the phone during an interview so it may be better to actually dress as if you were going to an in-person meeting. Keep your feet off the desk and do not walk around as you are talking.

• You may also want to consider posting a picture of the person you are interviewing with on the wall in front of you. This is a proven technique to make the call more engaging.

• Practice in front of a mirror. The more you smile, the more lively and engaging you will sound on the phone. If that makes you too self-conscious, call a friend and have them do a mock interview with you.

• Check your energy level. Get a good night sleep the night before and be alert on the day of the interview. This may mean getting up early to be able to drink a couple of cups of coffee or you may want to pop a mint into your mouth about 20 minutes before the conversation is to begin.

• Have a glass of water nearby in case your mouth gets dry, but do not eat or smoke during the interview.

• Just like in a face-to-face interview, keep your answers to two minutes or less.

• It is acceptable to ask the interviewer to repeat something they said once or twice but if you need to ask several times, you'd be better off asking if you could call back for a clearer connection.

• At the end of the interview, ask what the next step will be in the process and if they need anything else from you at this time.

• Send an email or letter within 24 hours thanking the interviewer and again reiterating key areas that are relevant to the position.

♥ Ronnie - Dating Coach

The First Phone Call in Dating

You met a great guy online (or so he seems) and are ready to talk on the phone. Just like with job hunting, this is extremely important. I cannot tell you how many men and women have messed up during the phone call and never got to meet because they didn't understand this is NOT a casual conversation.

My dating advice is to take the first phone call seriously. However, you don't want to have a serious conversation. What do I mean? This initial encounter serves as a way to vet your date:

1. Can you have a decent conversation?

2. Do you notice any red flags before you decide to meet?

Since the first objective is to have a fun conversation, you can't do that by firing off questions from your checklist. While acquiring details about a potential date is really your second objective, your first is to have a light-hearted conversation. You really can't do both at the same time. Don't think you can grill a guy before you meet him or on a first date either. That never goes over well with men.

When it comes to portraying yourself as a great catch and a fun date, you won't be able to show up like this if you focus on getting all your questions answered immediately. What can you talk about? Here's a list of surefire suggestions for topics that can easily start a fun conversation:

- Favorite foods
- Types of music he listens to
- Sports he follows
- Exercise he enjoys
- How he spends his free time
- Favorite vacation spots
- TV, movies and other forms of entertainment

On the other hand, I recommend you avoid the following subject matter because these are tough topics and can feel confrontational or too personal for a first conversation or a first date:

- Anything about his divorce (asking if he's divorced is OK)
- Past relationships and why they failed
- Religion
- Politics
- Work

Men do not enjoy being questioned intensely. Unfortunately, many women fall into this trap, which is such a shame. I refer to this as the difference between conversation and interrogation. Please remember that while you are trying to find out if he's a good match and qualify him against your list of criteria, it's a two-way street. He is also trying to decide about YOU. That's why, if you don't make the call fun and easy, you might not get a first date.

Don't worry, you'll get to ask him your questions. Keep in mind what works best is to weave them in among other topics during the first few dates rather than to shoot them off rapid fire. Put yourself in his place for a moment. I know women who have spoken to men on the phone who felt put off by invasive questions about divorce, how many dates they've had, and why they are still single.

What are you looking to discover during the first phone call?

- Do you like the sound of his voice?

- Does the conversation flow or is it awkward?

- Do any red flags pop up while talking to him? (He seems prejudiced, angry, boring.)

- Does he make you feel uncomfortable or suspicious?

- Does he seem friendly and have manners?

- Does he seem interested in getting to know you and asks you questions?

These are your most important "first phone call" concerns. Hold off on the rest of your burning inquiries; you'll get to those later. Following this practice allows you to enjoy the conversation and come across as a fun and easy person to be with. That's what most men want - a woman who is smart, fun, and easy going.

Last but not least, sound happy! The easiest way to do that is by smiling! Do your best to get comfortable even though the first call can be a little nerve-racking. Stand up and walk around to give you energy or look out a window at nice scenery to help you relax. A smile in your voice is very attractive.

Dating Lesson

My matchmaker friends talk about couples they try to match who never connect because they misuse the first phone call. They refer to this as "phone dating" and strongly advise against it. Too often the potential couple engages in an intense interview session to vet each other before agreeing to meet. Guess what happens? That's right - no date!

Nothing is easier than disqualifying a prospect. Saying no to a date is a breeze. The real test of your desire to find love is pushing yourself to go have a glass of wine or cup of coffee and meet new people. There are some things you cannot know without meeting in person. Chemistry is the biggest one.

When I was dating I met this guy, Ted, and we had the best phone conversation. We just clicked and had incredibly fun banter. I couldn't wait to meet him and was very excited. Then we met for a date and had absolutely NOTHING to say to each other.

I'm still not sure how that is even possible, but it happened. That was probably the shortest date in history because we could barely eke out a couple of sentences between the two of us. We just had no face-to-face chemistry. I never would have known this if we hadn't met.

On the other hand, I had a client, Sharon, who had a phone conversation with a hopeful blind date and immediately disqualified him because of a political comment he made. That snap judgment could have cost her. Synchronicity prevailed and she ended up meeting him at her friend's party one magical Friday night.

The two hit it off immediately and talked for hours. At some point during the evening, they realized they had spoken before. Sharon was so glad she'd been lucky enough to meet him in person to see how she had misjudged him. They were still happily dating last time I heard from her.

Don't use the phone call as your way of shortening the qualifying process. You could easily miss out on some great guys by harshly judging them or interrogating them and turning them off. Instead, simply see if you can have a short 20-30 minute conversation that is pleasant and then decide if you want to meet.

7
In-Person Interviews & First Dates

Beth - Executive Recruiter & Career Coach

As an executive recruiter, I help people prepare for interviews on a daily basis. The interview is the most critical part of your job search. It is the best opportunity to showcase your talents to prospective employers while also determining if this is the right place for you. The key is to strike a balance between talking about yourself while gaining insight about the organization, culture, hiring manager, colleagues, and duties of the position.

How does a job interview mirror a first date?

You have to strike this very same balance between talking about yourself and gathering information about your date. In this chapter, I'm going to show you how to have more success with both situations - the job interview and the first date.

A successful interview and first date should be an even exchange of information. Ideally you will ask 50% of the questions and so will your interviewer or date.

If the interviewer is doing all the talking, that may be a red flag as to how he manages others. And if your date doesn't ask you any questions, it might be a sign that he is nervous or more interested in impressing you than getting to know you.

On the other hand, if you're doing all the talking, you may be rambling, coming off as a flake, or a know-it-all, which is not good for business or dating. In general, men don't like super chatty women who don't know when to stop or ask a question. So, keep your answers short, maybe two-minutes in length. If the interviewer or your date wants more information, he'll ask a follow up question.

I have devised my own acronym for working with my executive recruitment clients – SCORE. The strategy behind each letter is described below to give you a full understanding of how this system helps with the job or love search.

The "S" stands for skills.

When interviewing, you want to mention the attributes you bring to an organization regarding education, special training, certifications, special projects, and daily responsibilities. Choose a few items on your resume and provide a more in-depth explanation so as to demonstrate your skills and expertise without having to say "I have experience in …"

The "C" is for culture.

Many people have enjoyed the daily responsibilities of their job, but did not like the company culture, which made them unhappy. That's why it's imperative to thoroughly research what makes the company "tick."

One way to research is to read as many LinkedIn bios from that company as you can, even if they are not from the same department. You are looking for things like longevity within the company, educational backgrounds, work histories, and overall presence of these people to give you an idea of the type of people who work at the company.

You can also ask the interviewer why so many people have been there a long time or why there are a lot of new folks. Two additional key questions to ask are:

1. "What would a typical day look like for me?"

2. "How much interaction will I have with others outside of my department?"

This is critical because if you prefer to keep work completely separate from your home life, you will not be comfortable working where every birthday is celebrated, company picnics are mandatory, and drinks after work are the norm. As an example, a friend of mine has worked at the same company since she was 19 years old and she is now in her 50s. She is constantly bringing food to the office to celebrate coworkers birthdays, anniversaries, etc. She also goes to others' homes for parties and dinners and she entertains them at her house. Even when I call the company and ask for her, the person who I speak to knows who I am even though I don't know them. Although I liked knowing some details of my colleagues when I worked for a major corporation, I would never want it to be that intrusive into my private life so I could not work for her company.

The "O" represents organization.

The hierarchy of the company is also important. Whom will you report to and how many other reports do they have? How many people are in your department? Whom does your boss report to?

Why is this necessary to ask? It goes back to the culture piece. If someone works for a Fortune 500 company with lots of resources including a large staff, it may be difficult to transition to a smaller, entrepreneurial organization which requires you to roll up your sleeves. In addition, no two companies are structured the same so you want to know how many steps from the top you'll be which indicates level of authority and autonomy.

For you, if you supervise others, make sure you know the titles of your staff and the number of people that report to them because a recruiter will ask you that question. It always amazes me when I interview a candidate and they hesitate because they can't remember a title of their own staff.

Also, don't get hung up on a title of a job. Companies are constantly coming up with "new and improved" titles so what one company calls a "leader" may be different in another company. Human resources used to be called personnel and now in some companies it is referred to as talent management.

The "R" is for results or your accomplishments.

During the interview, don't regurgitate what is on your resume verbatim. Instead, pick one accomplishment and explain it using different words. Be sure to insert metrics and clarify how you could replicate this result for the hiring company. A good statement is "I increased sales by 10% in three years." This statement is even better: "I increased sales 10% in three years by identifying a new target market and contacting them through an e-newsletter."

Another way to stand out from other candidates is to have a portfolio of some of your work to show or a leave behind for the interviewer to review later. The main objective here is to show that you have been successful in the past and can bring that same success to a new organization.

The "E" is for extra, which relates to pesky behavioral questions.

My clients often ask what is the benefit of these odd questions. There are several answers –

• Many hiring managers are not trained to interview, so they get suggestions from others for ideas of questions they should ask or they have read a book on interviewing.

- The interviewer wants to see how creative and quick you are on your feet.

- The questions are designed to catch candidates off guard so he or she will reveal themselves through body language. Facial and body movements can say a lot about who you are.

- It is the only part of an interview that is not about facts. The focus becomes your views, hopes, goals, etc. Asking someone what color they would be or what kind of television show character they see them as can be more telling than the balance of the interview or resume.

- This is a sneaky way to find things out that an interviewer by law cannot ask. If you are asked to describe what you do "off hours," you may mention that you coach your son's little league team so now the interviewer knows you have children and can discover if you are married.

How to Ace an Interview

1. Be prepared. The best way to have a successful interview whether by phone or in person is to be prepared. You need to conduct thorough research on the company, the hiring manager, and other items mentioned above. Then practice your answers to questions out loud.

2. Check appearance. Appearance is critical too so make sure your skirt is not too short when you sit down or that no cleavage shows when leaning over. For men, button the collar of your shirt and be sure your tie is not stained.

3. Solid handshake. The handshake is the only time you have physical contact with the interviewer. Women tend to use a "princess handshake" which makes you seem soft. Some men use the "death grip" handshake which can also put the interviewer off. Practice shaking hands and having good eye contact.

4. Watch your body language and don't fidget. Be engaging and personable. Smile often and nod your head to indicate you are really listening. Avoid touching your jewelry, hair, or clothing. I once had a younger candidate interview at one of the larger financial institutions. The feedback was that she had good skills but she stood three times during her interview with the hiring manager to pull her skirt down. Needless to say, she was no longer a candidate.

❤ Ronnie - Dating Coach

Why a First Date Is a Lot Like a Job Interview

I'm going to use Beth's SCORE formula to help you have a great first date with as many men as it takes to find "the one."

The "S" stands for skills.

When it comes to being a savvy dater, you'll need to develop your skills. What kind of skills do you need for dating success?

• How to strike up a conversation and end it without awkwardness

• How to gracefully deflect questions you prefer not to answer

• How to flirt using body language to let men know you are approachable

• What to say at the end of a date to improve your chances of being asked out again

• How to use your feminine charm to avoid emasculating your date

• How to enjoy meeting new people and take the pressure off each date

• How to handle rejection and build confidence

All of these skills will make your dating journey to find love easier and more enjoyable. The more well-honed this set of skills is, the easier time you will have navigating the emotional waters that come with the territory.

This is why I recommend dating lots of men. They don't all need to be your ideal man either. In fact, men who don't meet all your criteria are the best types to date early on because you won't feel as much pressure to do everything right. You'll be able to relax more and be yourself, which will help build confidence.

The more dates you have, the more practice you get which allows you to feel more comfortable when meeting someone new. As your comfort level increases, the more confident you'll feel and appear. Remember confidence is considered one of the most attractive qualities in a partner.

The "C" is for culture.

For dating, culture is about conversation and common interests. On your first date, your goal is to see if you can hold a decent conversation, and at the very least understand and enjoy each other's sense of humor. You might ask your date:

- "What hobbies do you have?"

- "How do you spend your free time?"

- "Do you prefer time alone, hanging out with one friend or socializing in groups?" to determine your date's social preferences.

These questions create the opportunity to talk about fun topics and lead to discovery of common interests.

What often happens with women who are out of practice dating is they become intent on gathering the information they want about their date as fast as possible. Sadly, they don't give a second thought to how that feels to the man. Dating is a two way street. Most men do not like to be grilled which means they do not want to answer your rapid-fire, probing questions.

If you aren't getting second dates, this is something to think about. Don't try to vet your man in one date. You'll push him away and you won't get the truth you want anyway.

Learning the art of conversation is a skill that will serve you in every area of your life. A first date is like a chemistry check to see if a second date is warranted. That's why you want to make the conversation light, relaxed, and fun.

Of course, there are important details you want to know, but like the Wicked Witch of the West in "The Wizard of Oz" told Dorothy so eloquently, "All in good time my dear, all in good time." You'll get more details with every date, but first you have to get a second date. Lighten up and make the conversation enjoyable!

The "O" represents organization.

With dating, structure relates to your dating agenda. Think about what your date wants. Is he seeking a something casual or lasting love? This is not easy to figure out right away. I have found asking men direct questions does not usually elicit an honest answer. Like a game of poker, most men don't want to reveal their cards too soon because it spoils the game, right?

When I was dating, I told men I was looking for marriage on the first date. Then I'd watch to see how the guy reacted. Did he squirm or look away? What did he say about marriage or relationships? What I learned the hard way was that some men will say anything they think a woman wants to hear to get into her pants.

This is where your feminine charm and ability to observe are far more effective. You can feel free to state what you want so your date knows your agenda. Simply say what you are seeking, a long-term committed relationship. Some guys won't ask you out again because they know they don't want what you want, even if they don't say so. That's actually a good thing because they won't waste your time. You won't scare away men who want a long-term relationship and the others don't meet your criteria, so you have no worries about telling men what you want.

Remember the purpose of dating is to gather information about the man to see if he has true potential as a romantic partner. This requires many dates with the same man and is not something that can be figured out quickly. You want to observe how he treats you, how often he calls and asks you out, how he treats others, talks about his family, his ex and more. You'll start to pick up clues by observing his behavior over time.

It's actually easier to weed out men who don't want what you want or don't meet your criteria. Be aware that you can't put your faith into what a man says. It's his behavior and actions that matter most. There is often a discrepancy between what men say and do. As a woman, your best test of character is to find a man with alignment between what he says and does. Saying the right thing is easy compared to following through and acting on those words.

The "R" is for results.

With dating, you hope your date results in romance! While interviewing for a new job requires retelling your accomplishments, being too business-like is anything but romantic. In fact, if you stay in your business head, you might create an air of competition, and nothing can kill romance like a man feeling competitive with you.

I'm not suggesting you can't be who you are, need to "dumb down," or hide your achievements. But I do recommend not focusing solely on this aspect of your life. You are more than your career. Men have to compete with women at work, so they don't want to compete when it comes to relationships. Down the road he will be supportive and you will swap work stories. However, at the start of things when you are making a first impression, tell him briefly about what you do and then move on to other parts of your life.

On the flip side, some women sit down with a man the first time and if he's a good listener, they will spill their guts about all the problems they face. This is not romantic either! Countless men have told me they are tired of women treating them like a therapist, pouring out their troubles on a first date. I agree! That is no way to get a man interested in you. He doesn't want to take on your problems.

Instead, you want to show your BEST side to make a good impression, just like on a job interview. Avoid discussing your ex, your divorce, your dating history, your online dating experience, or problems with your job, health, finances, children, or family. Just like you, men want a positive partner who is fun to be with. Your troubles will not be fun for him and they aren't fun for you. Save those conversations for your friends and family until you have established your relationship.

There are a couple of big reasons why you want to follow this advice. First, when you reveal your personal problems on a first date and never hear from those men again, you end up with lots of men who know your private details. That's not good! Your private life should only be shared on a "need to know" basis until a man has proven himself to be consistent and worthy of knowing that level of personal information.

Second, if you talk about your problems about dating or your ex, you are revealing that some men thought you were not right for them or undesirable. When your date hears how bad your ex treated you, you might not gain sympathy. It could actually have the opposite effect of repelling him. He might wonder why you put up with it or what you did that caused such poor treatment. While this isn't fair, it's human nature to draw conclusions like this.

Stories about your struggles are better off shared once he is interested in you because his judgment of the situation will be different at that point. The chances of him thinking poorly will be diminished because he already knows and likes you.

So, if you shouldn't brag about work or complain about your struggles, what can you talk about? Fun subjects like how you spend your free time, what new thing you are learning, books, movies, food, sports, etc. Talk about what brings you joy and see if you connect there.

The "E" is for extra pesky behavioral questions.

Sometimes on a first date, a man will ask you direct questions about your divorce or other private matters. You don't have to answer these questions or reveal anything that makes you uncomfortable. As I mentioned above, personal details about your life are a privilege shared with trusted friends. Feel free to brush off inappropriate questions by saying something like, "I'd rather learn more about you." Or, "Let's stick to positive topics for now. I'll tell you more as we get to know each other."

I've heard about men who ask all sorts of outrageous questions. Here were a few of my favorites:

- Will you wear a bikini on my boat?

- Do your bra and panties match?

- Have you heard about Tantra (an Asian practice for extending intercourse)?

Remember you don't need to answer anything. Feel free to laugh off a tough question or respond with something like, "Wouldn't you like to know?" Handling the situation this way is another example of feminine charm. You don't need to fly into a rage, telling him how insulting this is or inappropriate. Responding in a light-hearted manner will prevent unwanted arguments and help you save face. The softer approach will always serve you.

Keep in mind that when a man questions you inappropriately or brings up topics that aren't great first date conversation, he is revealing something about himself. Sexual queries tell you what he's interested in right away and let you know he's not looking for anything serious or long term.

First Date Prep

For dating, Beth's interview suggestions hold true as well. You want to prepare questions to ask your date, as well as your own answers to these same questions. When you are prepared and know what you want to say, you won't be thrown off or left "umming" your way through the response.

Naturally, you'll want to check your appearance and choose an outfit that is flattering and makes you feel alluring. When you know you look good, your confidence soars which is highly attractive. Please don't throw on any old thing. Or if you are arriving straight from work, think about what you put on that morning with your date in mind.

Eye contact and a good handshake make a difference for dating as well. Get used to the idea of hugging also because that is likely to happen on a first date. It could also happen when you first greet each other, and at the end of the date if things go well. Lastly, decide upfront whether or not you plan to kiss a guy on the first date so you won't need to decide in the moment. Feel free to turn your cheek to avoid a man's kiss on the lips. Creating your own rules helps you feel more in control of the dating situations. And of course you can always break your rules and kiss if that feels right.

Dating Lesson

Learn How to Talk to Yourself

Another important piece of dating wisdom is learning how to talk to yourself. Everyone has non-stop internal chatter going. When you are about to meet a new man, all sorts of ideas run wild through your mind. Calming your fears and quieting your mind will make dating easier and result in less anxiety.

You might not even be aware that you are talking to yourself. All that idle conversation is your brain hard at work, figuring things out and fretting about the unknown. In traditional coaching we call this "The Gremlin" or your "Inner Demons" who drag you down and hold you back. The good news is you can actually take charge and turn this around.

How you talk to yourself is nothing more than a habit. Your inner voice is a compilation of authority figures including parents, teachers, and mentors. Often you say things to yourself you would never say to another human being. Most people are cruel, lack patience, and can be extremely mean to themselves on a regular basis uttering comments like, "Who do you think you are?" or "That's never going to happen."

This voice is meant to keep you safe. It watches out for you by discouraging risk. The problem is without risk, how can you try anything new? You certainly can't date if you want to avoid taking risks. This is why you want to change your inner chatter to be more positive and supportive.

Here are a couple of exercises to try:

• When you notice your gremlin filling your head with fear about your date, stop and take a deep breath. Then say something supportive to yourself. For example, if you notice thoughts like, "He's never going to like me," switch gears and say to yourself, "I'm likeable. I'm fun and a great catch. He'd be lucky to have me." This is how you turn around those negative comments and build yourself up instead.

• Don't wait until you hear that negative stuff. Shift to speaking positively to yourself before you meet your date. Prepare an ego-building statement in advance that you can say to yourself before every date. Before you get out of the car or enter the building, recite (or read to yourself) your positive dating statement so you can enter feeling calmer and more self-assured. This works!

If you don't know what to say, try this statement below. Feel free to adjust the statement so it applies specifically to you. Make sure whatever you say, you feel good when repeating it - that's how you know it will work.

"I am an attractive woman who is a great catch. I am fun to be with and a pleasure to talk to. I have my own special allure and men find me attractive. I am easy to be with and loving and men recognize this about me. The right man for me is out there and is on his way now. If it's not this man, there will be others. Thank you in advance for an enjoyable date."

8

Behavioral Questions for Career & Love

(Questions Beyond Your Resume)

▪ Beth - Executive Recruiter & Career Coach

Usually behavioral types of questions are asked during a face-to-face interview, but that is not always the case so you must be prepared. The interviewer wants to see your body language especially facial expressions. A candidate who looks shocked or appalled reveals a lot regardless of how they answer the question. The point of this exercise is for the interviewer to gauge how quickly and effectively a person reacts when faced with an abnormal scenario or a difficult question. This demonstrates how you might react in a meeting, handle client interactions, or respond to a customer complaint.

If these types of questions are being asked over the phone, stay calm, and do not repeat the question. Sometimes that is a tactic to give yourself more time but it doesn't work as well in this situation. Instead, answer the question as quickly and creatively as possible. If you feel that you did not answer well, address it before moving on to answer the next question.

Behavioral Questions

• Tell me about two of your accomplishments and how those experiences would be a benefit to our company.

• What three words would you use to describe yourself?

• Tell me about a situation you feel you did not handle well at the time and what you did to correct it.

• What is an area you feel needs improvement? How would your supervisor respond to this question? Your subordinates? Your family?

• Describe your last supervisor. What traits did you like and dislike about him/her?

• How would you describe the ideal boss?

• What are the responsibilities in your present position that you really enjoy handling? What are the responsibilities in your present position that you don't enjoy?

• What is your management style? How do you communicate with your staff? If it is a global team, how do you handle cultural differences?

- Are you more of a morning person or afternoon person? Describe a typical day.

- How do you describe "being under pressure"? Give an example that has happened in the last six months.

- What motivates you at work? At home?

- What is the biggest misperception about you?

- What have you been criticized for in the last four years? Do you agree with the criticism?

- How do you like experiencing new things such as new places to live, new groups to join, new projects?

- What do you like to do when you are not working?

- What types of books do you like to read? What was the last book you read and why did you choose it?

- What has been the biggest disappointment in your life?

- If you could relive one experience in your life, what would it be?

- What is the most important thing you are seeking in your next role?

- What professional associations do you belong to? How did you choose them? What is your involvement with them?

- Forgetting about the position you are interviewing for, what would be the ideal next role for you?

- What kind of position would you like in five years?

- What does your garage look like? What would your neighbor say about your garage?

- What animal would describe you best? Why?

- How do you motivate people?

- Tell me something about yourself that is not on your resume that I should know about you.

- Who are the best people you recruited and where are they today?

♥ Ronnie - Dating Coach

Dating Questions for Engaging Conversation

With a first date, establishing rapport is much more important than qualifying a guy. It's about enjoying the interaction and finding common ground – books, movies, activities, hobbies, passions, lifestyle, etc.

To make the best first impression, avoid interview-like questions. What can you talk about with so many topics off the table? Here are suggestions to help you learn about each other in a fun way without any pressure.

- Are you more of a morning, afternoon, or evening person?

- What is your passion in life?

- Do you like to try new things? What was the last new thing you tried?

- What do you do in your free time?

- What would you do on a rainy Sunday afternoon?

- What types of books do you like to read? What was the last book you read and why did you choose it?

- What is your favorite movie?

- What kind of movies do you like?

- Tell me one fun thing you did in the past you'd like to do again.

- What are you looking for in a partner?

- What type of vacations do you like?

- Where did you go on your last vacation?

- What's your favorite restaurant?

- What's your favorite kind of food?

- What kind of pizza do you like? Thin or thick crust?

- What is your fondest high school/college memory?

- Do you enjoy sports?

- Do you follow any teams?

- Do you play any sports?

- What kind of music do you enjoy?

- Do you go out to see live music?

- What are your top three activities?

This is not a checklist but suggestions to get a good conversation rolling. You would never ask all of these questions on one date. Pick out five favorites to use in case the chatting slows down. These questions are designed to get someone talking about things they like so you can see their passion and find similarities Naturally you can follow up with your thoughts and respond to what he said. Be sure to have your own answers to the questions you plan to ask.

Dating Lesson

Recruiters and hiring managers ask behavioral questions to help them identify past behaviors that can predict future performance. For dating, the process is far more intuitive. Answers to these less pressurized inquiries will help you gain insight into how your date feels about certain things, reveal different viewpoints about life, and discover common interests.

How you ask these questions can change the kind of answers you get. Your delivery means everything. The last thing you want is for your date to feel like he's on a job interview! That is so unappealing.

Instead, a first date should be a casual exchange of information between two people - in other words, fun conversation. Your manner should be light-hearted, with humor when possible. Maintain eye contact, but feel free to look away too. You want to mix it up because if you look too long into his eyes, it can feel intrusive or even aggressive.

Another way to gather information about your date is to pay attention to his body language. This is a strong indicator of how a man is reacting to you and your questions. If he gets flushed, stutters, looks away often, or seems uncomfortable, this reveals a lot more about him than his actual words. Pay close attention if it happens after you ask a personal question it may indicate he's hiding something on that subject.

If he leans in when you are talking and smiles, this can suggest he's really interested in what you are saying. Same thing is true if he cocks his head to one side and asks a clarifying question about something you just said. Men often take up space to show command of the area, which is territorial. A confident man might sit with his legs apart and his hands behind his head. But if your date doesn't display this behavior, it doesn't mean he's not confident, so don't worry.

I caution my clients about making snap judgments, ruling out a man for the way he answers one particular question. Unless his response is immoral, rude, or obnoxious, cut the guy some slack. Anyone can get nervous on a first date. He may get his words mixed up or hesitate. If this problem seems consistent throughout the conversation, then you can re-evaluate if you want to date him, be friends with, or run for the hills.

Let's face it – anyone can have an off day or not feel well. Where you can, give men the benefit of the doubt since conversation the first time may not reflect his true personality. That's why I suggest you date a guy you aren't sure about three times to see who he really is.

If after the first date, you aren't sure if you like him, but don't dislike him either, then go on a second date. If the second date is also inconclusive, give him a third try. After three dates, if you still aren't sure what you think or haven't started liking him, you can move on knowing you gave him a solid chance.

This happened to me with my husband. For our first date we had a beer and the conversation flowed well. The second date we went to dinner, but he seemed tired and didn't have much to say. I was disappointed and felt unsure if he'd even ask me out again. I also worried he might be boring and not the right man for me. Then our third date was truly magical!

Months later his sister told me he didn't feel well on our second date, but he didn't want to cancel and was too shy to say anything. He just wanted to muddle through it. I could have easily kicked him to the curb, thinking he would never do. Thankfully, I gave him another shot and he's the man I married in May of 2000.

Give men a chance. Judging them harshly is easy. Being patient and open to getting to know a man can help you connect with your ideal match who wasn't so perfect for a moment in time. Give any man who seems okay three chances before you count him out. It worked for me.

9
Handle Rejection for Job Hunting & Dating

▪ Beth - Executive Recruiter & Career Coach

Unfortunately rejection is part of the job search process. There are many reasons that a candidate is not selected for a position and surprisingly a lot of times it does not even have to do with you. It is hard not to take it personally, which is why you need to develop a thick skin.

In today's world, it is more than your credentials that lead to being the final candidate. It takes a certain persona and a bit of luck to land a new job. The process starts when a recruiter views your LinkedIn profile and then requests your resume. Some people do not make it past this stage because their image does not fit what the company is seeking. I can't tell you how many times I have seen poorly written resumes, boring formats, or dated terminology (for example, "References Available Upon Request" is old school!). Many candidates post a photo on LinkedIn that is too casual or worse, ten years out of date. Some companies won't even consider you as a candidate if you don't have a photo posted on LinkedIn.

If you make it to the interview phase, keep in mind you'll likely be interviewed by several people, and they may ask you back a few times. Many companies do not have a formal training program for their hiring managers as was mentioned before so they might ask questions that are not relevant to the position, are inappropriate, illegal, or so crazy you wonder if you want to work there. So be prepared and expect that anything can happen.

Not only does the way you answer questions matter but your body language will also be taken into account. So sit tall, smile, and don't fidget. Be careful when talking about past events and your current boss. No one wants to hire a Negative Nancy or Ned, so stay positive no matter what.

There are countless reasons why you might be rejected for a position. This may happen because you seem overly nervous or answered a question incorrectly. The interviewer might not be paying attention and as a result, you did not get a fair assessment. They may be distracted by a multitude of other things or feel that they should not have been part of the interview team and feel they are wasting time. It could be a million things that for the most part, are completely out of your control.

Another reason you may be rejected is when an internal candidate surfaces. Many companies post their jobs internally, but there is one Fortune 500 company that I work with that never does. Instead they rely on internal referrals from senior managers. The problem is senior managers may not be aware that a member of his staff would be open to relocation or a new challenge. Once the internal candidate becomes aware of the search, they are often selected. The truth is they are already known entities, which involves less paperwork, and demonstrates to employees that the company does promote their own.

The search process can be very long especially when companies are looking at candidates that will need relocation. Patience and a willingness to be open-minded are important qualities for a candidate to portray, but it does wear on you after a while. It's hard to know how frequently you should check in with the recruiter or hiring manager to find out what the status is. Too much contact makes you seem desperate and too little may signify your lack of interest.

I suggest sending an email every ten days unless you are told the search is on hold or that there will be a delay for a certain amount of time. No matter how much time has passed, it's better to appear upbeat and understanding when you receive the next status update. Whatever you do - DON'T DISAPPEAR! It is understandable that you may be annoyed with how the search is going but candidates who do not respond to phone calls or emails tarnish their reputation, which will be remembered for years to come.

DO NOT start acting desperate or even threaten a recruiter. When I told one candidate he was no longer being considered, he insinuated it was due to his age so he was thinking about a lawsuit. The reality was he had come off as a pompous jerk so he was no longer being considered and by acting this way later just confirmed my suspicions about him.

If, after the interview, you feel that you did not answer a question well or did not give enough detail, mention that in your thank you note. I also suggest if you made it to the final rounds, but were still not selected, stay in touch with the hiring manager.

Keep in mind that rejection is part of life. A lot of it is beyond your control so you might as well accept that right now. You certainly can learn from your mistakes, but if you truly feel you did everything right, realize there are other factors including personal opinions and prejudices that might get in the way of you being hired.

Whatever happens, don't beat yourself up. Be kind to yourself. You worked hard researching the company, getting your interview outfit ready, writing a thank you note, etc. Now is the time to do something nice for yourself. Go out for a good meal, work out at the gym, or buy yourself a small gift. If you still feel bad about the situation, seek out others through career transition groups, your friends and family, religious leaders, or career coaches who can empathize with you for a short time. Then, get back on track with a positive attitude and a new perspective.

♥ Ronnie - Dating Coach

Dating Rejection and Recovery

Rejection is not only part of life and the job hunt, it's a big part of dating. There is no way around it. If you are dating to find love, you are going to be rejected by some men. You'll also reject plenty of guys. That's the way it works. If you want to avoid rejection, you simply cannot date.

When I decided to get serious about finding love, I actually had no interest in dating. I just wanted to meet my husband. Obviously, that's not possible! Many people want to skip steps so they can get to the good part faster, but that isn't real life is it?

I ended up meeting lots of men, dating 30 different guys in 15 months. Number 30 is the man I married. Did I experience a lot of rejection during this journey? You bet I did! The truth is most of the men rejected me. Out of the whole group, I only rejected five. Most of the men didn't ask me out again or disappeared after one, two, or three dates.

However, I learned how to handle all that rejection and not fall apart. Don't get me wrong, I didn't become impervious or unfeeling. Not a chance. I felt it all. Yet, I figured out how to view rejection and shift my perspective so it didn't hold a tight grip on me or keep me from dating.

I'm going to share my proven methods for handling rejection and staying positive on the dating journey. These tips really work and have worked for thousands of women like you!

One of the best things I did was discover how to talk to myself about rejection. Much of the pain you feel is what you inflict on yourself internally. Once again, your own inner chatter can be vicious and unrelenting. The end result is that you make yourself miserable. Do you catch yourself with thoughts like:

- Why didn't he like me?

- I'm never going to find anyone.

- I have bad luck dating and with men.

- What did I do wrong?

- Who would like me? I'm too old, out of shape, heavy, flat, dull, wrinkled, short, tall, etc.

- I'm not lovable.

These thoughts are not accurate or based in truth. They might relate to a moment in time or a few bad experiences. So, why do you allow yourself to believe these ideas are the whole truth and let them erode your self-esteem and bring nothing but unhappiness? Most of the techniques I created to handle rejection are ways to shift this harmful, negative internal chatter that can be emotionally crippling.

Don't let your gremlin win. Remember you are in charge, not the negative stuff floating through your mind.

1. "Who's Next?" Thinking

I discovered there was a big advantage to meeting many men and having plenty of dates. Dating a lot of men meant there was always someone new on the horizon. When one guy didn't work out, I learned to ask myself this empowering question, "Who's next?" I can tell you that made things a lot more fun and exciting. It helped me look forward in a positive way to the next man I might meet.

One night I met my date in an upscale restaurant bar. We had connected through a personal ad so we didn't know what the other person looked like. We had described ourselves so we could find each other at the bar, but those descriptions are sort of general height, hair color, etc.

As I approached him and verified he was in fact, Scott, my date, he looked me up and down quickly. Then he looked at his watch, looked back at me and said, "I've

JOB SEARCH = LOVE SEARCH

got 15 minutes. What do you want to drink?" I gulped and froze.

I'm not usually known for a shortage of words, but found his reaction to me rude and shocking. Even though my instinct was to say something rude back, I thought a drink would be helpful right about then. He bought me a beer and we chatted briefly before going our separate ways.

I was shaking even after the beer as I walked back to my car. His reaction felt so mean and harsh. I got in my car and sat for a moment, thinking about what happened. I was so sad, and started feeling hopeless that this was never going to work and I wasn't going to find love. Tears flooded my eyes as I let those horrid thoughts about myself take over.

Then I was surprised by a positive thought that popped into my head. I suddenly remembered I had a first date with another man the very next night! This sparked a whole line of thinking that had never occurred to me before.

- Who the heck is Scott anyway?

- I didn't find him attractive either!

- What makes him so great?

- Scott doesn't know a great woman when he sees one because I am wonderful!

- Who is the next man I can meet?

After that, everything shifted for me! This was very exciting and I turned those false, debilitating thought patterns around to regain my positive outlook. There are always more men to meet!

"Who's next?" is a very empowering question to ask yourself and a wonderful way to look at dating. It helps you remember that there is so much more to dating than any one particular man. There are many more where he came from. Don't let that one guy bring you down because he is NOT the only man available. The Universe is an abundant place and there are better men waiting to meet a wonderful woman like you.

2. "Meant To Be" Thinking

After the sting of rejection, take a little time to feel your feelings, but don't overdo it. Instead, it really helps to realize that if that man didn't choose you, he's simply NOT THE RIGHT MAN. The Right Man will know you are a great catch and pursue you until you are his. He'll want to spend time getting to know you.

Reminding yourself of this crucial fact can save you hours and days of suffering about some guy who got away and rejected you. It's a more positive way of using the classic, "It was meant to be" thinking. The truth is, if it was meant to be, it would have worked out. Since you aren't dating him, what was meant to be was that you'd move on and find a man who IS attracted to you and wants to be with you.

3. He Did You a Favor

When a man rejects you after a couple of dates, the first date, or even after a phone call, he has done you a big favor. How can I say that? Because it's totally true. Look at it this way – he didn't waste a lot of your time trying to decide if you were the right woman for him. He departed quickly, freeing you up to go on and meet another, better man.

As with "meant to be" thinking, the right man for you WANTS to stick around. So, you can conclude he must not have been the right man which means, he actually did you a favor by opting out early.

I had a client once who had an hour-long first phone conversation with a man she thought was perfect. Towards the end of the hour, he asked her to remind him how many children she had and their ages. She told him and he sounded disappointed. He told her that he was sorry but didn't want to date a woman who had three young children.

She was so upset she called to tell me she was giving up dating! I tried to calm her down and explain that he was being honest. Should he have figured this out earlier in the conversation? Maybe, but I can't fault a man for being honest. He didn't want to waste any more of her time because he knew this situation could not work out.

When a man rejects you quickly, keep this sensible thought in mind. He did you a favor by not wasting your time. It didn't take him 3-6 months to realize this was not a good match, which would have been a heck of a lot more painful.

4. Positive Neutrality

If you are going to date, you do have to toughen up. I tell my dating coaching clients not to fall in love with a profile, an email, a text, a phone call, or after a single date. You are more worthy than that.

Dating also requires managing your enthusiasm. If you appear overly eager to a man, he can read this as desperation which is a HUGE turn off. The same is true if you start to initiate contact by texting, emailing or calling him asking him out, or inviting him places. During the initial six dates (at a minimum), it is best to avoid contacting him first. Men are funny about having their "space invaded." What works better is to let men pursue you and ask you out for the first few dates. This also helps you monitor his interest level.

You want to keep a positive outlook while at the same time remaining somewhat neutral. Consider this line of thinking about a new man, "Okay, he's handsome and really interesting, but I'll see how things go." Finding love is rarely instantaneous. It blossoms like a rosebud unfolding its petals and nothing will make that happen faster than the natural scheme of things.

To hold a positively neutral mindset means that you are happy to meet a new man and happy to date him. But don't shut down other opportunities or start thinking "He's the One!" until you have more evidence this is true. Even if you have wild feelings right away, that doesn't make him the right man.

The man you date and consider for a potential mate needs to show you consistent interest over weeks to know he could have lasting potential. You also need to see how compatible you are and discover if you have the same dating agenda. Some men will date you consistently but want to keep things casual, where others are open about looking for a mate. These are not details you can learn in a date or two. It takes time to get to know someone.

Now you have four proven methods to help you recover more quickly from rejection. Sometimes you can bounce back right away without skipping a beat. Other times it might take you a few days. That's okay. Just don't let rejection shut down your heart or keep you from getting back out there to look for love.

Everyone goes through this trauma. As I mentioned at the start of the chapter, being willing to date lots of men actually makes bouncing back easier. Yes, you become skilled at pulling through and see that you are more resilient than you ever imagined. This builds your confidence and makes you brave to continue the search.

Knowing that you won't end up in a puddle on the floor after a bad date is very empowering. You really are strong and can persevere, especially now that you have these proven methods for handling rejection.

Dating Lesson

When you are rejected, keep in mind it's not always about you - it might have nothing to do with you at all! A guy may think he's ready to date, but in reality he's not over his divorce yet. This can show up in many ways. He might want to play the field, seem non-committal, inconsistent, or not sure of what he even wants in a partner.

One of my dating coaching clients, Sally, was dating a man who was very attentive and seemed to really care for her. After a couple of months, he mentioned his sister had seen a picture of the two of them and remarked how she looked like his ex-wife. This left an impression on Sally and she started to realize he was just looking for a substitute for his ex-wife. She started noticing that when she didn't mirror what his ex-wife would have done, he would slip into a mood.

On the flip side, one male client chose NOT to date a particular woman BECAUSE she looked like his ex-wife! In this case, he did let her know this right up front versus months down the road, so she wasn't left wondering what happened. Many men won't say a word though, but that's no reason to start blaming yourself.

Another factor that contributes to rejection is timing. When Beth moved to Rhode Island, she was eager to start dating. She went on a few dates but quickly realized she wanted to spend her time getting her house in order and her kids feeling comfortable in their new surroundings. After a year of focusing on her home and family, she was then mentally ready to commit the time and energy to dating and looking for love.

Life Can Get in the Way

Unexpected problems may derail a potential relationship or even end it completely. Issues with children or elderly parents who need assistance can require a lot of time and be very stressful. When you add working full time, doing chores and errands, and trying to exercise, there are just not enough hours in a day.

Squeezing dating into your life may seem like a nice escape but not everyone can get her head in the game no matter how much she claims to want a relationship. A man may seem eager, but then his follow up lags and he disappears. At first you might be understanding, but over time resentment builds. He might feel guilty when you discuss this and want to do better. Sometimes, he's just not capable of changing anything or being there for you more and so it ends.

Keep in mind this important foundation for finding love; before you start dating you have to love yourself first. Being in a good place about yourself will help ease the pain of rejection you face. Take time for self-care like pampering, exercise, massage, reading personal development and dating books, all of which build your feeling of self-worth and self-esteem.

Realize that when it comes to dating, many things happen that are beyond your control. Loving yourself first will help you cope with rejection or disappointment. You'll learn to recover faster and take these things less personally. Everything you do to build confidence and take care of yourself helps to minimize bumps on the road of your dating journey.

10

Negotiate Your Job Offer & Love Life

Beth - Executive Recruiter & Career Coach

Many job seekers do not think about negotiations until they receive an offer. That means they do not spend the time researching and contemplating what they are really worth in the marketplace BEFORE they start the job search. Instead, many accept either what is offered and do not negotiate for more or use a simple formula like an increase of 10% on their cash compensation. This is how you may miss out not only on more money in your pocket but also perks like more vacation time, stock options and grants/restricted stock, and telecommuting options. That's why salary negotiations can be so tricky!

The first step in the process is to realize you bring a talent and value to the new employer. A company hires you because you possess an expertise they lack which is why they need you. Unfortunately, many job seekers see it differently and may also really need a job. While that may be true, all of your experience and skills do have a value in the marketplace. For this reason, make a list of all your accomplishments, not just the ones that you have on your resume. By doing this, you can better determine how much you are worth to a potential employer and determine what your compensation should be.

The next step is to create a personal budget if you do not have one. Without this, you cannot properly judge the impact of the salary package you are being offered. As mentioned below, you may reduce costs by taking this job but you may also encounter some increases. For example, maybe you had a five-minute commute before and drove your car. Now you will have to take a train so there is that expense, plus parking fees. Jot down every expense you have each day for a week and then analyze which costs will still be the same and which ones will change when you take a new position.

You should also consider other reasons besides money to take the job. There have been many studies showing money is not the key motivator for changing jobs. Instead, the main reasons are the direct supervisor you will report to, learning new skills, exposure to a new industry or functional area, or a passion for the cause, product, or service. Job satisfaction may come at a price but if you really enjoy what you do, then you may be willing to make concessions in your compensation package.

The research phase of negotiations is very critical and will take a good deal of time to do it. There are various books and websites to guide you in understanding your true value. Be sure not to just review base and bonus information but also long-term incentives and other perks like education reimbursements. In addition, if there is a relocation involved, you must verify the cost of living differentials for housing, schools, taxes, municipal fees, and other expenses like the price of gasoline.

The industries you are pursuing also have their own compensation parameters. All these factors can influence the final numbers, so determine the whole package and figure out where you can make concessions if necessary. Don't forget about items you may be eliminating or reducing by taking this position such as:

- Shorter commute time means less maintenance and gas for the car.

- A dress code of business casual vs. suits means smaller dry cleaning bills.

- An on-site cafeteria or an on-site gym can save you money on food and gym membership.

- Options to work from home reduce commuting costs and wear and tear on your vehicle.

These sites can be very helpful for conducting your negotiations research:

- www.salary.com

- www.salaryscout.com

- www.payscale.com

- www.vault.com

- www.glassdoor.com

- www.salaryexpert.com

There are also a number of books and articles to assist with determining compensation. The Department of Labor Statistics and industry associations are also sources of information. If a recent college graduate is seeking compensation information, the National Association of Colleges and Employers (www.naceweb.org) is a good place to start.

Once your research is gathered, talk to contacts in your network to get their thoughts and feedback. Choose people that recently landed jobs in your desired field as well as others that are the decision makers in hiring decisions. If you do not have a robust network, use LinkedIn to reach out to people who may be able to assist you.

Next, develop the bottom line numbers that you will need to change jobs and be sure it aligns with your personal budget. Take into consideration everything mentioned above and also parts of your budget like entertainment that could be scaled back if needed to take a position offering a great learning experience but a lower salary.

What type of negotiator are you? You may not realize this but you probably engage in some form of negotiations almost every day. This includes asking for a discount on a product or service from a company, buying a car, and even haggling with your child about a curfew or a cookie after dinner.

Regardless of the scenario, there are intrinsic characteristics about yourself that define what type of negotiator you are. According to the book, Bargaining for Advantage by G. Richard Shell, there are several negotiation styles or strategies. It is possible to use different strategies depending on the situation, but most people tend to fall into only one category.

• Avoidance. You do not like to negotiate so you just don't. About 20% of jobseekers do not counteroffer when they are seeking new employment for this reason.

• Compromise. With compromise, each side comes to some agreement that delivers equal gains for each party. For example, a company might offer a $50,000 base salary and 10% bonus and you counter with a $60,000 base and 20% bonus. The end result is somewhere in the middle like a $55,000 base plus a 15% bonus.

• Accommodate. Being too accommodating is not practical in job search negotiations because as the job seeker, you are going to miss out. The company is not doing you any favors by not giving you what you want, so why would you agree to a compensation plan that doesn't work for you? The reality is that being nice and accommodating puts you in a position to lose the most. Some human resources professionals and hiring managers may try to bluff you by saying, "We never have someone at this base salary for this role, but for you we are going to do it." Believe me, they have looked at the numbers and had discussions about what parameters they can offer the final candidate.

- Competitive. The competitive strategy will probably work better in some industries than others like financial services. However, be careful as some maneuvering using this approach may seem unethical or underhanded and the hiring company may get turned off and rescind the offer. Companies expect job seekers to be competitive, but it must be done in a way that does not come across as abrasive and/or unrealistic. It is also not a good idea to accept an offer and use it as a way to get a raise from your current employer hoping they will try to retain you.

- Collaborative. The collaborative approach is the most creative and can be the most time consuming. You'll brainstorm ideas and resolve tough issues together coming to an amicable offer. Suppose the base and bonus the hiring company is offering is fair but you are going to lose your spouse's salary with relocation. The company is willing to provide outplacement services for your spouse, yet that might not be enough. You may counter by asking for a sign-on bonus and a consulting assignment for your spouse for a set period of time or until a full-time role is secured. Counter offers with other innovative ideas may continue but this takes time and may need buy in from higher ups as well.

Gender and cultural differences can also be factors in the negotiation process. Men tend to be more assertive, while women tend to want "everyone to be happy" so they are often more accommodating. Different cultures also have unwritten rules and protocol that they adhere to and those must be recognized.

Regardless of your style, gender, etc., the critical component, when possible, is to be a good listener and watch the body language of the person making the offer. You can negotiate more effectively if you pay close attention to inflections, word choice, etc. Keep in mind that all of us bring expectations to the table when we negotiate and we also bring prejudices. A male job seeker may feel he has the upper hand with a female human resources professional so behaves as if he is in charge. Never underestimate the person on the other side of the negotiation table.

If you are the type of person who is nervous while negotiating, I suggest writing down what you want and practice saying it aloud. The more confident your delivery sounds, the better your chances are for receiving the compensation package you want and deserve. In addition, recite your desires to a trusted adviser or friend and have him or her work with you on more powerful wording and key phrases to emphasize.

As you prepare, try to anticipate how the other person is going to react and plan your proposal accordingly. It will be a different scenario if you are negotiating with the hiring manager directly or with a human resources professional or executive recruiter. Ideally the one who holds the purse strings is the one you want to negotiate with. You absolutely have leverage because they want to hire you and have invested a lot of time and money to find the right candidate. Use that to your advantage.

If you are unemployed, don't think that you cannot negotiate. Again, keep in mind you possess valuable skills that a company is willing to pay for. It may be a bit trickier to determine your compensation package if you have been out of a job for some time but by conducting extensive research you will be well prepared to negotiate a fair salary and perks. Companies want to retain their employees because of the significant costs required to hire new ones. Don't forget, there is also a cost associated with downtime while a new employee "gets up to speed" in their new position. As a show of good faith, companies will often negotiate with an unemployed candidate.

Now that you have done your research, identified what type of negotiator you are, and established some deal breakers, you are ready to negotiate. If possible, let the hiring company make the first offer instead of you telling them what it would take for you to make a move. That's how you find out where they are willing to start and don't short change yourself by offering too low a figure.

Through the external or internal recruiter or someone else, they already know what your current compensation plan is so it's to your advantage to let them make the first move. Although they may have relayed to you a range on what the position pays, you may know through your resources that the compensation is low or that other perks are customary for this line of work. Do not react immediately to their first offer. Tell them that you need a day or two (no longer!) to think it over.

Contact them with your counter offer and expect that they may want time to reply as well. Patience is essential because if you appear anxious or desperate the negotiations will not work in your favor. Hopefully it will only take one or two counter offer rounds for you to get the appropriate compensation.

♥ Ronnie - Dating Coach

Negotiations in Dating

Negotiation - express your needs and stand up for yourself from the beginning. It gets harder later, so don't wait.

You may be wondering, "Negotiations in dating? What is she talking about?" But as Beth pointed out, you negotiate across many areas of your life every day. The main point here is to be sure you don't hold back from sharing your opinion, letting your date know what works for you, or asking for what you want.

Women often hold back in an effort to be nice or accommodating. Yes, you want to be easygoing and easy to please but not at the expense of your true desires. You need to be reasonable of course and avoid seeming overly demanding. There is no question this is a delicate balancing act.

Know that every couple interacts differently. The way you negotiated with one man might not work with another since every person is unique. You'll need to go through some trial and error as you learn how to communicate with a new partner.

What kind of things will you be negotiating? There's a broad range of situations that can crop up including:

- Where to have dinner
- Which movie to see
- Who will drive further when you meet somewhere
- The amount of notice he gives you to schedule a date
- How long to wait before sleeping together
- How much texting you are willing to do

When you step back and think about it, there really is a lot of compromising in any relationship. You might not have thought about it that way before but that doesn't change what is required to get along and form a bond.

What I share with my dating coaching clients is not to be afraid to speak your mind or ask for what you want. However, positioning and delivery of that message changes EVERYTHING. Regardless of how much equality we have achieved between the genders, men are still men and women are still women. Even if you are a total chick-in-charge and master of your destiny, learning how to communicate with men has major benefits.

Let's say a man you started seeing often calls at the last minute to ask you out. This doesn't work for you because you like to plan ahead or need to line up a babysitter. He needs to know this, but how you tell him is the art of negotiation and feminine charm once again. You could be direct and say, "Calling me last minute doesn't work for me. Next time I want at least three days notice." I can tell you that kind of delivery will not land well with most men because it is more like a business deal than a relationship conversation.

The better way to deliver this message is to soften your approach. Start with something nice because positive feedback smooths the way for a request. "I'd love to see you, but I'm not free tonight. Being spontaneous is fun, but I have to line up a babysitter. Next time maybe you can let me know sooner."

If you find texting with him is becoming overwhelming and you want to have more phone conversations, you can text, "Call me." A less direct approach that can be highly effectively is to make a suggestion and again soften first with a positive statement, "I'd love to hear your voice. Let's talk on the phone."

There is no rejection or admonishment for the man when you express yourself this way and you'll avoid crushing his ego. Trust me, this makes a huge difference in how a man hears what you say to him. When you offer a man the information about what works for you, a man who is genuinely interested and capable will likely follow your request.

Another way to handle too much texting is simply to not answer his text immediately. If you always respond right away, you are reinforcing texting behavior. Waiting might help him get the message. On the other hand, texting by its nature is an immediate response type of communication and a man can get the wrong message if you don't text back. You could always text that you are in the middle of something and will get back to him later.

Plenty of single women tell me they don't have time for anything but the direct approach or they can't be bothered figuring out the softer approach. That may be true, but it makes me wonder, "Do you want him to be thoughtful and caring with you?" If this question makes you open to the idea of a little positioning and positive reinforcement, that's good news! You want to treat him the same way you want him to treat you right?

Every relationship needs to be nurtured. Dating is not like a business deal to be closed with a vengeance and feel victorious afterwards. A romantic relationship builds over time to create an emotional bond that will hopefully last for years to come. It is worth investing in. Take the time to respond in a way that appeals to a man rather than just complete the communication.

When a client comes to me with something she wants to say to the man she's dating, we create a script. To be honest, this is something I am very familiar with because I had to learn to communicate more carefully myself. As I dated 30 men to meet the man I married, I found out the hard way that my direct, business-like approach did not go over very well.

As I learned to negotiate and communicate with my feminine energy, I got better at conveying a message and making my point with gentle suggestions. This allowed the men I dated to feel more positive about me so I could avoid appearing demanding (even if that is my true nature). All the while I was asking for what I wanted, taking care of my needs and learning to express myself!

I am a huge fan of asking for what you want and letting a man know what works for you. When a client comes to me and is afraid to bring up a subject or give a man feedback, I explain how a healthy relationship requires this. You have to learn how to negotiate if you want your romantic relationships to progress.

When you hold back and remain silent, you will feel taken for granted, unappreciated, or at the mercy of a man's whims. None of these feelings lead to a solid relationship that can grow and improve with time. If you are afraid to express yourself and tell him what isn't working, you are not giving him a chance to discover what he is capable of or demonstrate his love for you.

You might be thinking, "But what if he doesn't get my point of view or doesn't want to make changes? What if I make him mad?" As a dating coach, my perspective is you might as well find out early if he cannot accommodate any of your wishes. If he's not capable of some compromise, you might as well know right now versus wasting time with the wrong man.

That's why your first disagreement is so incredibly important. You need to know if he will make an effort to work things out. How does he communicate with you? Does he shut down or is he willing to talk it over? His willingness to negotiate with you lets you know how much long-term potential he really offers. The right man for you will hang in there to settle a situation for mutual satisfaction. He wants you to be happy which is why the right man makes this effort.

Dating Lesson

The key to negotiations in the business world or dating is that everyone wants to feel good about the outcome. In other words, it should end up as a win-win situation. Otherwise there could be problems down the road that are irreparable such as breaking up or rescinding the offer of employment.

You need to know what your date is unyielding or feels flexible about. A deal breaker for you might be not dating a smoker or needing someone who likes to exercise as much as you do. Those are obvious desires. But what happens when some of the things you want are not as clear cut? You may want to go out with friends once a weekend and see your man the other night. Maybe you'd like him to cook dinner for you occasionally rather than going out to eat when you had a rough day. How do you broach these topics without hurting his feelings or causing a fight?

The solution is to communicate your feelings by beginning with a compliment. Start by saying "I love the chicken Marsala you made two weeks ago. It would be great if you could take over cooking me a nice meal like that once a week, especially when I am really tired."

You have to be sensitive to what he wants too and at the same time avoid being a doormat. Women often want to "take care of their man" which is fine to a point. Always being available, changing plans to accommodate him, and doing things that you hate will not work for you in the long run. Overextending the services you provide like sewing on a button, ironing, or even cooking, can create resentment when the man you're dating doesn't reciprocate in a balanced way.

Men like to feel wanted, but they also have a "hunter mentality." When you do everything he wants even if you don't want to, that sends a message that you are desperate for a man, have no needs of your own, opinions, or preferences. I doubt that's true. Either way you lose ground and end up appearing less desirable. Men like confident women who know their own minds and live their own lives.

Epilogue

We hope we have provided you with the best possible tips and insights to help you find the right job and the right man. Apply these proven tools and suggestions to make your journey easier. There is no question that you deserve to achieve the career and relationship success you dream of. Keep going until you get what you want. We believe in you and know you can make it happen.

Cheering you on!

Beth Carter and Ronnie Ann Ryan

Acknowledgements

Debbie Fay of bespeak presentation solutions

Jim Hopkinson of Hopkinson Creative Media, LLC

Melanie Gosselin, Libby Raccio, Patti Fritz, Carol McManus and Jennifer Carozza.

Bios

E. Elizabeth "Beth" Carter, a Certified Coach, launched Beth Carter Enterprises in 2011, a thriving business that encompasses executive, business, and career coaching, workshops and presentations, and the DISC, Motivators, 360, and Emotional Intelligence assessments. She serves as a "thought partner" for executives and middle managers of small and Fortune 500 companies, business owners, and people who want a more fulfilling career.

In addition, she is President of Carter Consultants Ltd., an executive search and research firm she founded in 1991. Beth has been published in The Huffington Post, East Bay Newspaper Group and quoted in articles including Yahoo Education and the book *Mogul Mom*. She is also a public speaker and workshop facilitator for companies, universities, leadership conferences, women's events, and career transition groups. www.BethCarterEnterprises.com and www. CarterConsultantsLtd.com

Ronnie Ann Ryan, MBA, CCC —The Dating Coach for Women Over 40—has helped thousands of successful midlife gals attract the magic of love since 2002. Whether you've given up on love or are frustrated by dating, Ronnie's Dating GPS system offers the guidance you need to find love faster. She dated 30 men in 15 months to find her adorable husband and married for the first time at 43.

Ronnie is a certified coach who has been featured by the BBC, ABC, NBC, and Fox News, NPR, Fox News Magazine Online, Huffington Post, eHarmony, YourTango, Digital Romance, and MORE.com. She has written several books including *MANifesting Mr. Right* and *Why Can't I Find Love?* and has contributed to a number of others. Get her free book *7 Dire Dating Mistakes That Keep You Single* at www.NeverTooLate.biz/gift